MINK TRAPPING.

A LARGE MINK.

MINK TRAPPING

A BOOK OF INSTRUCTION GIVING MANY
METHODS OF TRAPPING—A VALU-
ABLE BOOK FOR TRAPPERS.

———

EDITED BY
A. R. HARDING.

———

PUBLISHED BY
A. R. HARDING
COLUMBUS, OHIO

By A. R. HARDING PUB. CO.
ISBN 0-936622-16-4

CONTENTS.

LIST OF ILLUSTRATIONS.

G. R. Harding.

INTRODUCTORY.

WHILE there are some excellent mink trappers, no one man has studied out all the methods, for the conditions under which the trapper in the South makes his largest catches would probably be of little value to the trapper of the Far North, where snow covers the ground the greater part of the year.

Conditions along the Atlantic are different than the Pacific, and as well the methods used by thousands of trappers along the Mississippi and its tributaries differ from the Eastern or Western Coast trapper, for the mink's food is not the same along the fresh inland waters as the coast or salt water.

The methods published are from all parts of the country, and many experienced trappers tell of their best methods, so that it makes no difference in what part of America you live, something will be found of how to trap in your section. Most of the articles are taken from those published in the F-F-G with slight correction.

A. R. Harding.

MINK TRAPPING.

CHAPTER I.

GENERAL INFORMATION.

Mink are found in nearly all parts of America living along creeks, rivers, lakes and ponds. While strictly speaking they are not a water animal, yet their traveling for food and otherwise is mainly near the water, so that the trapper finds this the best place to set his traps.

The mink is fond of fish, rabbit, squirrel, birds, mice, etc. In some sections they eat muskrat, but we believe they prefer other animals, only eating muskrat when very hungry and other game is scarce.

At certain seasons scent seems to attract them while at other times the flesh of the rabbit, bird or fish will attract them. The trapper who makes mink trapping a business should have various kinds of traps and sets for them, such as steel traps, both bait and blind sets, as well as deadfalls.

Mink, while small, are quite strong for their size and very active. While a No. 0 Newhouse will hold them, the No. 1 is usually considered the proper trap.

As already mentioned, mink travel a great deal near water, so that the place to catch them is close to the water or in the water. If you notice mink tracks near the water, in some narrow place where the bank comes nearly to the water, or a rock or log projects nearly to the water, carefully dig a hole the size of your trap and an inch or more deep, covering with a large leaf or a piece of paper first. Then place a thin layer of earth removed over leaf or paper, making the set look as natural as before. The dirt from the hole for trap as taken out should be thrown in the water or to one side. One of the great secrets in mink trapping, especially blind sets, is to leave things as near as possible as they were before the set was made.

There are various shades of mink—some quite dark, others brown, pale, and some cotton. The greater number, however, are brown. In the Northeast, Maine, etc., mink are not large, but the color is rather dark. In the same latitude some ten or twelve hundred miles west in Minnesota and Manitoba, Canada mink are larger but not so dark. Still further west on the coast of Washington mink are again smaller, being somewhat similar in size to the Maine mink but much lighter in color. Throughout the central section such as Ohio, Indiana, Illinois, Iowa, etc., they are larger than the Maine mink but smaller than Minnesota. In color not near so dark as the Eastern or Maine mink.

The cotton mink is found principally in the prairie and level sections. In general appearance it is much the same as a pale or light brown mink, but on blowing into the fur the under portion is white, hence cotton. Such skins are worth much less than the brown and dark ones. In fact, for years cotton mink sold for 10 to 50 cents.

During the past years the value of mink skins has varied a great deal. The number exported annually varies from a couple of hundred thousand to a half million skins or more. This gives but a faint idea of the annual catch, for large numbers are used each year by American manufacturers.

There has been a great deal said about mink climbing trees, many being under the impression that they could not or did not unless leaning trees. This is a mistake, however, as trappers have tracked them in the snow up straight and good sized trees. They will also occasionally tree when close pressed by dogs.

Mink can be tamed if caught when young but are rather treacherous, and should never be handled bare handed. A few attempts have been made to raise them for their fur, but so far no great success has been achieved. The raising of mink will no doubt be undertaken from this on by many, especially if prices remain as of late,

2

A MINK TRAPPER.

for when skins sell for several dollars each the business looks promising. No man should engage in the buisness unless he knows something of their habits, etc.

In the states bordering on Canada mink become prime usually by November 1, while south along the Gulf of Mexico they do not "prime up" until about December 1 and begin to shed by February, so that the extreme Southern trapper has only about two months when the skins are at their best. In the central sections such as Pennsylvania, Ohio, Indiana, Illinois, Missouri, etc., the skins are prime by November 15 but begin to get pale in February if the winter is open.

While some fur bearing animal den up during severe weather mink do not, and the trapper, even in the Far North, will find mink on the go every night.

As mentioned elsewhere, the greater per cent. of the mehods published in this book are taken from the FUR-FISH-GAME, an illustrated monthly magazine, of Columbus, Ohio, devoted to hunting, trapping and raw furs. New trapping methods are constantly being published in that magazine, as experienced trappers from all parts of North America read and write for it.

CHAPTER II.

The favorite haunts are along marshy shores of lakes, rivers, creeks and other swampy places, and where muskrats are plenty there you are almost sure to find mink. When hunting for mink the best place to find them is in old muskrat holes near the point or end of an island, and the next best place is under bridges where the approaches have been filled in with stones or logs; there are other places not so good, such as stone piles, heaps of fence rails, hollow logs, under large stumps, and have even found them under snow banks where I knew there were no holes at all.

The principal food of the mink is fish, birds and their eggs, frogs, mice and small snails, and have had them partly eat muskrat while in my traps. I do not know wheher he can kill a muskrat or not, never having seen him do it. No doubt there are many other things upon which he feeds of which I do not know, but these are the principal ones.

The mink is an animal of peculiar habits, sometimes remaining near his burrow for weeks at a time, and then suddenly disappearing and not returning for as much as seven or eight days, and all this time he is roving around in search of food, running all night and lodging in the best hole he can find when daybreak comes, and can often be seen in early morning or in evening at dusk.

The mink is not so hard to trap if you know his habits; when you find he has left his burrow

LOOKING FOR FOOD.

do not take up your trap, for he will **surely be** back in a few days; when you come to a place where a mink has laid up for the day (that is, in a temporary burrow), do not trap on the route he has already traveled, for when he comes out he will go straight on just as if he had just looked in and come out, but set traps and bait; when he comes out he will be hungry and is sure to be your mink.

In going from place to place mink often **travel** over the same route, as between two

GOOD SIGNS.

swamps or ponds, and at times there is a well
defined runway through the grass; this habit can
be studied in winter when snow is deep, and
also when swimming from the mainland to an
island or from one island to another; they will
nearly always land in the same place.   Another
thing, when finding a burrow look around, and
if you find his dung heap you may be sure he
lives in that hole; minks' dung can be told by
mice hairs and other remains, and if he is feed-
ing on fish altogether looks the color of silver or
the scales of fish.

I have had a world of experience trapping
but very limited at catching, says an Arkansas
trapper, yet plenty of both to be fully capable
of solving the question as to whether or not
mink are afraid of the scent of iron.   It is simply this.   Some mink are positively afraid of it
and some are positively not so.   The experience
with one mink that walks into the properly concealed trap and the other old fellow who makes
the short but invariable curve around the same
properly concealed trap is positive proof of this,
and few if any experienced trappers have not
had this experience.   Either use a scent the
mink likes or boil your traps in ashes.   Clean,
wipe and keep dry, and you have a better chance
on land at both kinds of mink.

My favorite water set for mink is as follows:

Roll a good sized log (the longer and larger the better) to within six inches of the water's edge of a stream, pond, or lake, leaving a strip of land about six inches deep, allowing water to come in and touch log. Throw mud you remove far away. Don't step on or leave finger or paddle prints on your strip of land, which is certain to become a mink path.

As soon as tracks indicate this, from land side step on top of log and place trap in the place you have made and parallel with log, allowing water to cover well. Staple to log low down and under water between trap and log, or if you desire to use sliding pole, place upper end of same under log at this same prepared place and under water. This log is better than the same set at root of tree, rock, or stump, for the reason of its convenience to stand or kneel on and avoid leaving sign while making set, and because when mink reaches middle of his narrow path he does not like to back out, take deep water, or climb over the log.

Should he have any suspicions, should he jump clear of your little water neck, make wider and place two traps or use the same width trap in soft mud at either edge, and when he jumps he will land deep in your trap. I caught the largest mink I ever saw with the trap in mud at edge this way and he pulled the staple and took the trap, but I found him the same day and the trap, a Newhouse No. 1, had him by the hind leg above the hock.   The old fellow had been jumping my little neck of water, so I fixed the trap to his convenience and he lit in it hard.

CHAPTER III.

SIZE AND CARE OF SKINS.

Mink hides handled right bring from a fourth to a half more in market than the same hides handled indifferently, says an old Iowa trapper and buyer. Now I will state it more plainly. Take a medium sized mink, a male one if handled right will be, when stretched properly, from 20 to 22 inches long, and from $3\frac{1}{2}$ to 4 inches wide at the tail, tapering gradually to the nose.

Take the same hide, stretch it over a shingle tapered to a point being 6 or 8 inches wide at base and a foot long, you will get just half as much for it as the first one.

I have bought small mink hides about 8 inches long and 6 inches wide at the base—just as you would stretch a muskrat. Take the same hide, stretch it 15 or 18 inches long, and you have added 25 per cent. to the value of the hide. I shipped two large mink hide a short while ago. They were near of a size and color as could be. One was about 12 inches long, the other about 22 inches and well handled otherwise. One brought 100 per cent. more than the other.

I take common laths heavy as I can get, saw

NICELY HANDLED WISCONSIN SKINS.

them in two in the center, plane them smooth,
taper the ends of the two round the edges, make
a tapering center piece, stretch the hide over the
two outside pieces.   Draw the hide down as far
as you possibly can. See that the nose does not
slip off the end of the boards. Now tack the
hide on each side of the tail, putting in 4 tacks,
allowing room for your center piece.

Now you are ready for your center piece.   In-
sert it at the bottom, press it through gradually,
but be careful not to tear the hide from the tacks
that you have already driven in. The center
piece will not always go through the full length.
The size of the mink regulates that part of it.
One must have different sizes of boards or laths.
Now turn your hide over, pull down the legs
of the mink as tight as you can and tack, using
several tacks. I use large tacks No. 12 three-
quarters of an inch long, being sharp as needles.

Most trappers use the one piece sretching
board, as they claim the three piece too much
trouble. If the one piece is carefully made,
planed on both sides, and about three-eighths
inch thick, it is a good board. A one fourth
board after being planed on both sides is very
good.

In this country there are two varieties, which
some naturalists have supposed were distinct
species; one small, dark-colored, common in the

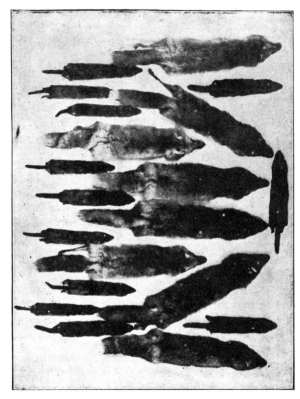

SOME PRIME N. E. SKINS.

Northern and Eastern States and Canada; the other larger, with lighter-colored, coarser and less valuable fur, common in the Western and Southern States. The dark-colored variety measured from eleven to eighteen inches in length from the nose to the root of the tail, and has a tail from six to ten inches in length.

The lighter-colored is large and is found in the states of Iowa, Minnesota, Dakota, Manitoba and adjoining Canadian provinces. It has been known to reach a weight of five pounds.

Trappers claim they have often secured pelts, without over-stretching, that were 25 inches long, $4\frac{3}{8}$ inches at root of tail and $3\frac{1}{8}$ inches at neck. This measurement being from root of tail to end of nose. From tip of tail to end of nose 35 inches. A few instances of even larger skins are fairly accurately established.

In the Northeast the skins are much smaller for instead of an occasional five pound mink one that weighs three is considered large. Owing to the fine fur and darker color it is worth as much if not more than skins larger, but caught in a more open section, such as the Dakotas, Iowa, etc.

In the states of Ohio, Indiana, Illinois, Missouri, etc., mink are not so large as Northwestern but larger than Eastern, yet are not worth as much money owing to their color not being so good.

In the states bordering on the Ohio River as well as Missouri, Kansas, Nebraska, etc., there are some cotton mink. In size they may be as large as any in the section, but the under fur is light, in fact often white. This greatly lessens their value, so that a "cotton" mink is often classed as a No. 3 or No. 4.

LARGE IOWA MINK.

When it is taken into consideration the various shades of mink, dark, brown, pale and cotton, and sizes from the different sections, to which are added Nos. 2, 3 and 4, it can be seen that to know all about the value of mink one must be in touch with all parts of the country.

Many have asked for a standard size by which to grade mink—large, medium and small.

The standard to be based on prime skins of course.

At first such a plan looks reasonable, but after looking at the suggestion from all sides it does not appear so.

In the first place prime, large mink vary in weight from 3 to 5 pounds, depending in what section caught. The five pound skin, usually from an open country, is pale and not so finely furred as a 3 pound one from the Northern New England States or Eastern Canada.

Again, were mink graded by a standard size, they would be over-stretched.

A dealer who we believe tries to treat all fairly submits the following measurements for the three sizes—large, medium and small:

Large, 22 inches long, 4 wide at tail, $3\frac{1}{2}$ at neck.

Medium, 18 inches long, $3\frac{1}{4}$ wide at tail, $2\frac{5}{8}$ at neck.

Small, 14 inches long, $2\frac{3}{4}$ wide at tail, $2\frac{1}{4}$ at neck.

The figures are from root of tail (tail not measured) to end of nose.

The measurements as given are intended to be general, including skins from Southern, Central, Western and Northwestern sections, with the exceptions already noted, but at the same time it must be kept in mind that all skins the same size are not worth the same.

It is a good idea to stretch the pelts as soon after removed from the animal as possible. If allowed to lay around for hours the pelt will be hard to stretch to its normal size.

If you find a mink drowned and thoroughly water soaked, take it by the head, just like you were cracking a whip, then by the hind legs and crack it the same way. The mink will soon be dry. If muddy it should be washed first.

Pelts should not be put on the boards when the fur is wet. They should also be removed as soon as thoroughly dry, that is, after the skin will not shrink. They should be left on boards from three days to a week, depending on the weather. Do not turn after removing from boards, but have flesh side out.

CHAPTER IV.

GOOD AND LASTING BAITS.

Animals are not afraid of smoked baits, and in the early and late parts of the trapping season it is a positive benefit to slightly smoke the bait; it lasts so much longer than fresh meat and hangs on to the bait stick until almost the last shred, and if an animal turns from the trap house without biting it, it is because he is not hungry.

The baits I have found the most enduring and most likely to tempt an animal are—first and always the muskrat. All animals, that is bear, mink, fox and marten will bite at this bait when they will not consider any other. For a bear trap, use one whole rat, take out the inside (because the inside will cause it to decay quicker), have the rat slightly smoked, just enough to stiffen the meat, then have a sharp pointed stick, about three feet long, run the stick through the two thighs, up along the back bone, through the neck stopping at the skull. Plant this in the back of your bear trap house and you have one of the best inducements for a bear to catch.

For mink or marten traps a smoked rat

makes five good sized baits, neck and head one;
each quarter one. Do not throw away the tail.
It stands in the same relationship as a tidbit
to an animal as a beaver's tail does to a trapper.
Therefore at the trap where you want an extra
inducement, twist the tail about the rest of the
bait and tie it to keep in place.

During the very cold months partridge and
rabbit meat keeps good a long while in the hard
frozen state, but as an all round lasting bait for
mild or cold weather, good for either mink or
marten, I have used with great success both the
windpipe and tail of the ox. The tail has, of
course, to be skinned while fresh, and I cut off
a ring or two of either the windpipe or tail and
run a sharp stick through each piece, and carry
them in my bait bag with the sticks in. When I
want one for a trap I pull out the stick and the
hole is there ready to place on the proper bait
stick. A tail will make ten generous baits, like-
wise the windpipe.

All fish bait is good for mink, but the majority
decompose so quickly that unless hard smoked it
drops off the bait stick in a few hours and is
eaten by the mice on the ground, or very soon
disappears by the action of the earth and evapor-
ation. As a lasting fish bait (unsmoked) I have
found the sucker or carp the very best; they are
a fleshy fish with no inside to speak of, and a

very tough skin. One of about twelve or fourteen inches long will give sufficient bait for ten
traps.

In setting mink traps along the shore of lake
or river I take the fish whole in the canoe, and as

CAUGHT IN MIDWINTER.

I set a trap cut off a section with my belt axe,
beginning with the tail. Each bait will be an
inch or an inch and a quarter broad lengthways
of the fish. You make your bait stick very sharp
and run it through crossways of the section,
piercing the skin on both sides. Long after the

flesh part of the fish has rotted and fallen away, the skin ring will be yet in evidence shrivelled up dry on the stick, but yet useful as bait.

In using partridge or rabbits for bait, it is very much towards their lasting powers to not remove the skin or feathers. Cut the section you want with a very sharp axe, run your bait stick through the portion of meat and plaster down close on top all the feathers, hair or skin and tie securely if in mild weather. If in cold weather, all that is necessary is to place each bait stick, primed, out of doors over night, and the next day you can carry them in your bait bag like so many knots.

In conclusion will say that a few drops of oil of anise is the best alluring scent I have found for mink. A final word of advice. Unless your traps in water-set always have a tossing pole, otherwise when you visit your line you may have the chagrin to find only the paw instead of the animal. As the minister says, one more word. If it is your intention to return on your tracks when visiting your trap road, be sure and clean out, bait and reset each trap as you go. In mild weather or towards spring, animals run as well in daytime as at night, and I have often, by observing this rule, found on my return at different times almost all kinds of animals caught while I was at the other end of the road.

CHAPTER V.

BAIT AND SCENT.

The mink is very hard to catch, as all or most all experienced trappers tell us, so therefore we must believe them says an experienced Canadian trapper. Some say that mink are afraid of human scent. In one sense they are but in another they are not as I will prove to you in the following paragraph:

While I was trapping on Twenty Mile Creek in Ontario I had an occasion to go my rounds very early one morning. I had not gone far before I ran onto a large mink track, and as the snow was only here and there in small patches I did not follow it. I returned the same way to get a skunk I had hidden, and on reaching this particular spot I saw as before, my tracks going one way and Mr. Mink's another. I never thought any more about it until I came to the next patch of snow, and there were his newly made tracks beside my own, and some were discerned in the same prints as I had made, so that must prove that he wasn't afraid of human scent there. If that mink had been afraid of human scent he most certainly would have avoided my tracks.

but as it was he saw me coming and hid somewhere until I was past.

I do not say that a person can drop a trap

NORTHWESTERN SKINS.

down anywhere, set any old way, and catch
mink; but I do say that it all depends where the
human scent is. If a man sets a trap and han-

dles it with his hands or any other foolish thing, he will catch but very few mink.

My way of setting a trap for a mink is this: Find a den or hollow log in the vicinity where mink tracks are seen. After you have found the place where you intend setting your trap, set it in the following way: Cut a hole in the ground at the entrance shaped like a straight stemmed pipe, only make it large enough for the trap to set in nicely. After that, set the trap, twisting the spring around to the same side of the trap as already excavated, and taking the dirt you have the pan, placing the trap in the place you have taken out, cover the trap with it, being careful not to let any lump or pebble lay at the base of the jaws, as it prevents them from closing tightly, and your mink may get away.

For bait, take the tail, front and hind legs of a muskrat, also a small piece of flesh, or better yet the entrails, and place them in the hole, being careful not to set it too close, but close enough so that the mink will have to step on the pan of the trap. It is better to have it too far back than too close, as you then run a better chance of getting your mink. Also have some musk or some reliable scent, and put a few drops on a stick a short distance from the trap. After all of this be very careful in brushing out all signs, and make everything look as natural as

possible, depart, and I know from experience
that you can catch a mink, providing you follow
the directions above.

In order to trap very shy animals use no bait
of any kind, but set your traps where they are
sure to go and you can capture the shyest mink
says a Maine trapper. The places where mink
are sure to go are into holes, dens, hollow stumps
and logs, and to make a success you want a trap
set at all the places. If there isn't any, make
some any time in the summer for the coming
season.

The right size and best kind of trap for mink
is the Blake & Lamb No. 1. Have them free
from rust and foreign odors, as mink have keen
smelling organs; boil them in ashes and water,
also boil them again in a kettle filled with fir or
cedar twigs, and after they are dried and when
hot rub them all over with beeswax, and when
set cover carefully and fasten to something
movable.

In the fall of the year use no scent, but in the
spring when they are running around use their
own musk, mixed with fish oil and salt to preserve it. This is my way to trap mink without
bait, and I have captured large numbers of them.

I claim that animals are their own best scent

If experience is worth anything I am sure of it. About the first trapping I ever did (1877) I ran out of mink bait and came across a rivulet running into the main creek and mink track in plenty. Well, what was I to do? I must set a trap. I took a piece of the hind quarter of a mink. Being a green hand at the business I did not know whether it would work or not. But the next time I visited my trap I found out the plan was a success, for I had Mr. Mink safe and sound. Ever since I have had occasion to use the same for bait.

Another illustration I will give which proves beyond question that this theory is a correct one: In 1878 I set a trap in a hole in the bank, the water not freezing all winter, but ran a stream over the trap, out of the hole. I used no bait. But I believe I caught every mink coming that way. Every mink caught of course would freshen up the place with his musk. The result was 15 mink. I believe other animals are the same; but skunk and civet are not so particular what they eat; anything half decomposed or rot- en will answer.

The civet is very troublesome when they find your mink trap. In setting in water (he will not go in water if he can help it) he will make a hole at one side and get your bait in spite of you. At other times he will crawl over all your stagings and reach in, like a monkey, apparently as limber as Indian rubber, and get your bait. In dry land sets they walk right into your trap and you can't get rid of them.

A few words about scent. I never did believe in mixing a lot of stuff together as some say, says a Canadian trapper. Now if a mink is at-

TRAPPER'S "SHACK."

tracted by the odor of fish oil or the scent of muskrat musk or of blood or the scent of the female mink, that does not say that we should mix them all together and expect it to catch every mink that comes along. Would you expect the mink to distinguish the smell of each of these substances when they are all mixed together? If we like chicken, sweet potatoes, chocolate cake and mince pie, would it make it better to mix all these things together? I don't think we would like it.

As for the fox, the very best scent or decoy is the matrix of the female fox, as has been de-scribed so often, but it is hard to get. Next to this I think comes skunk essence and it should be sprinkled around quite freely, as the fox is not afraid of it, like some trappers are, and it also helps to kill the smell of the iron of the trap. Now don't think by this that you should rub it on the trap. Just sprinkle it around the trap.

But none of these scents will attract an ani-mal as far as some seem to think, and I find that one of the most important things is to find where animals use and set your traps near these places. Of course you must study the nature and habits of your game or you will not know how to set the trap after you find the place. Then set your traps carefully, work hard, keep your eyes open, use reason and good sense, take care of your furs and you will be successful.

For mink I use a No. 1 or No. 1½ trap. The latter is preferable. For scent that obtained from the scent bags of the mink or weasel, mixed with anise oil, is the best decoy I ever used, says a Minnesota trapper. This scent is found near the root of the tail in two round bags about the size of a pea, and is a yellow liquid smelling very strong.

After setting the trap I scatter feathers around and over it. The mink, seeing the feathers and scenting what he supposes to be a weasel, will dig up the whole works looking for something a weasel has overlooked, and he is mighty lucky if he don't get in the trap. Canned sardines make good mink bait, and the sardine oil is good to mix with the scent in the scent bottle. Skunk scent and feathers attract and allay suspicions of all bird eating animals.

CHAPTER VI.

There is one place on my line of traps where I have caught six mink, says an Iowa trapper. I have no doubt but what this particular place is on their regular crossing place in going from one stream to another. I have a few good places but they do not equal this one. At these particular places I do not remove my traps during the entire trapping season. I find a man gets fooled quite easy at times by putting in traps at places that look extra good, when, in fact, it proves to be no good at all for mink. I often read of trappers who say to set traps at hollow trees, in hollow logs, and every place where a mink is liable to go. Well, a mink is liable to go any place. Also just as liable not to go, too. Now if you should place a trap in all these places you would have traps strung all over creation.

In my locality after a mink leaves a ditch or stream you cannot tell what direction he will go. Perhaps he will start across some farmer's field down between two rows of corn. Now I expect some of these nights Mr. Mink is going to take a run down through Farmer Jones' cornfield. He is liable to. Shall I place a trap between every row of corn? In my locality with snow on the ground they travel through fields more than any other place. I will tell you boys, I have three pet sets that I use, and which I stay just as close to the streams with as I possibly can, for the condition of the weather is such at most times that it would not pay to change the location of traps.

Some trappers will tell you that if a mink will throw his scent where he is caught you will get another one soon at the same place. Well I do not believe it, except from the female at mating time. I think when an animal throws a scent it is a danger signal.

Many trappers have told me that a warm night was the night to catch mink, because that was the time they ran most. That don't go with me, either. It is just because mink can smell bait better on a warm night, as the old trappers around here hardly ever set without bait, and think it is a wonder that I can catch mink without bait. In fact, mink run well on cold and disagreeable nights, just as well as on warm nights. I make it a point to have my traps in the very best condition previous to a change in the weather, no matter what the change may bring, there will be lots of mink on the move during the change.

Now boys I am not going to advise you to

make any particular set, but if you have two or three good ways, stay with them. They will bring good results. A man can spend lots of time trying to do something with some fake set and perhaps neglect some better sets during this time. A few good sets, well handled, will surely bring good results.

If I am to judge results from the conditions in my locality, I will say that fifty traps are too many. Twenty-five gives a man plenty of work here. During snowy weather you can set your traps with northeast east, or southeast protection and it is all right, until the wind gets to the northwest, then look out, for you will have some digging to get your traps in good condition. By that time the wind is in the south. Then it begins to thaw, then the water soaks through on your traps, then by the time you get around again they are frozen up solid. Then how a fellow wishes for more weather with a "sameness" about it.

An Eastern trapper says: My favorite set for mink is the water set. I find a place where the water don't freeze up, and if there are any stones around I lay a stone on each side of the stream, and then I get a flat stone and lay it over the two stones. I place these alongside the stream, making a hole like when the water comes out.

Then for a bait I use fish, brook trout if I can get them, or most any kind of fresh water fish. I put a piece of fish back in this hole so it lies in the water and set traps in entrance, and you are sure to get most every mink that comes along.

A GOOD MINK STREAM.

This set is for November, December, January and February until about the last part, when running time begins. Then I like the runways best, and you will find them under driftwood and along banks where the water has washed the bank so the trees standing on the edge have leaned over and made a hollow under the bank.

4

I have taken a good many mink this way and also with the water set. I took twelve mink last year that I kept, and had six get away by gnawing off their feet under the jaws of the trap.

The following is from an Indiana trapper: Here is one of the many mink sets I have been successful with: Go along a creek, find a log, one that is somewhat crooked will be better, as some part of it will sink below the surface of the water, roll same into the creek and tow along to a place where the water is two or three feet deep, take a strong wire 6 or 7 feet long and fasten to the under side and to one end of the log, fasten the other end of the wire to a stout stake and drive down solid near the middle of the creek.

Now find a place where the water stands above the top of the log, and chop out a place for the trap deep enough so the trap will be 1 or 2 inches under water. Now take some mud and smear over the fresh cut place so it will have an old appearance. Now set your trap and cover with a few water soaked leaves and a few pinches of mud. This set should be made where the water does not run too swift. Muskrat will bother this set some, as long as there are any near, but they are troublesome about most any water set for mink.

The fur bearers here are fox, mink, skunk,

opossum, raccoon and rats, and none of them plentiful, writes a Tennessee trapper.

I will tell you how I captured a shy old mink that had run my line of traps for two years. I had made up my mind to catch him or trap on the balance of my days. I set my trap in the spring where he had been wading; the first night he threw the trap and that seemed to make him shy of the spring.

I took a piece of muskrat and nailed it to a root above the trap, and the second morning I visited my trap I had a crow, not mink, and the mink had killed the crow by biting him through the back of the head.

That made me more determined than ever to get that mink. I arranged my traps all nicely, and the third morning I found a muskrat and he was cut up badly by the mink. I took the fresh carcass of the rat and rebaited again, and the fourth morning to my surprise I had another crow.

It seemed from the amount of tracks that they had fought a duel and the crow had come out ahead, for he was still alive. I fixed my trap all back again and the fifth morning had a fine muskrat.

Well, I had about given up all hopes of catching him at that place so I decided to move my set 200 yards up stream, where there was a log projecting out over the water 2 feet above the water, where he traveled under. There I gouged a hole back in the bank one foot back so the water would flow back in enough to cover the trap, and I baited with a fresh partridge, and the next morning I found my mink. Now boys, this does not look as if they were very shy of human scent, does it?

First find a den where they have been going under the ice or where they have been eating a dead rabbit or chicken says an Iowa trapper. Next I select my traps, Newhouse No. 1 or 1½ or Hawley & Norton 1½. I examine them to see if they are in good order. When setting at a den or where they have been eating some dead animal, cover with leaves, feathers or snow; fasten to a stick that can be dragged a short distance. I bait with chicken, rabbit, birds and mice. Fish is also good. Brush away your tracks and do not approach too close. If the traps are undisturbed, I leave them for a week. Frequently mink do not come out every night.

When setting where they go under the ice, I use a No. 2 Jump Trap. If the water is not too deep, lay two sticks in the bottom of the stream about two inches apart. Between these I lay bait, generally mice. Set trap, and fasten it to a stick on top of the ice. Cover trap with moss and leaves and you will generally get him, or, at least, that is my luck.

I will always remember my first mink. I found the den. They went under the ice and the hole was below the water. I set my trap carefully, baited with sapsucker and the next morning I had him. Set trap back and caught another one.

CHAPTER VII.

INDIAN METHODS.

Oftentimes while walking through the winter wood I find the track of a mink, that starts or ends in a brook or pond, says a New England trapper. To set a trap in this case, if the snow is light, I do as follows:

First, I use a drag around the woods where the track is seen. To make this I kill an old hen or rooster, split it open, and mix equal parts of fish oil and the juice that comes with oysters. If the track is very old, I add an equal part of oil of assafoetida, and put the mixture inside the hen, leaving the entrails in and sew it up loosely. Then I tie it to a rope, and starting at the point where the track leaves the water, drag it through the woods, not very far, ending in the brook again. At several places along the line I secrete traps, exactly in the path made by the drag.

A mink, striking the scent will follow it, and, there being no bait to scare him or arouse his suspicions, will run along the track until he gets into one of the traps. This is a good set to use in woods where a bait would mean having your

traps lifted by John Sneakum. I don't know
how it will work with others, but I have had fine
success with it, especially in the cases of old
"bait-shy mink."

Here is another set shown me by an old half-
breed Indian. We were in a light canoe, and
were paddling up a little reed-fringed brook,
from ten to thirty feet wide. In the weeds were
several muskrat houses. As it was spring, they
were all finished and the rats were no longer
working on them. The old man set two traps on
the house, and barely under water. Then he put
a few drops of the scent that is found in a sack
just under the root of the mink's tail, on a leaf
on the very top of the muskrat house; and then
placed a small piece of muskrat with the fur on,
beside the scent, fastening it with a skewer.

He said, "mink, come 'long and smell 'nother
mink an' muskrat on top house. He clim' up,
get caught, an' all drown good." "But," said I,
"muskrats will climb up too, 'cause you've got
muskrat meat for bait." "Oh-h-h no!" he chuck-
led. "Muskrat he heap 'fraid of mink. We
have mink to-morrer-wonca, numpaw, yowha,
yawminee mink (1, 2, 3, 4 mink). You see?
Then you no call ol' In'jun big fool." Sure
enough next morning he had shagipee (6) mink
to show for as many sets. The principle was
that the muskrat wouldn't climb up, for he

would see the fur and smell the mink scent, and think it was a mink.

Mink often follow muskrat trails, especially in the fall before the snow comes. To set a trap

INDIAN TRAPPER.

in the trail would mean to catch a rat, and make a meal for a mink; so I post a rooster's head about two feet from the trail and set a No. $1\frac{1}{2}$ trap under it. The rat isn't likely to leave the trail for the head, but the mink will, unless he is hot after muskrat.

When brooks unite and form a "Y" there is often a little sand pit left in the crotch of the "Y." I hang a piece of muskrat meat with mink scent on it upon a small stick leaning out over my trap, which is set in two or three inches of water, and staked out so as to drown the mink.

An Indian subscriber of the Hunter-Trader-Trapper and who writes of his experiences occasionally to that interesting magazine, in one season caught with dog and trapped in Northwestern Pennsylvania 104 mink. The name of this Indian is John Lord, and he has trapped as far west as California. The illustration shows him to be a young man. The picture shown here was taken in 1905 when he was hunting and trapping in Pennsylvania.

The 104 mink were caught during the season of 1905-6, and as the pelts were high then it can be seen that he makes considerable money. The fact that he caught that number is pretty well established by several well known parties. John is an Iroquois and a good fellow and trapper.

CHAPTER VIII.

MINK TRAPPING ON THE PRAIRIE

As there has not been much written on mink trapping on the prairie, I will give a few hints for the benefit of young prairie trappers, on trapping mink, says a Minnesota trapper. In the first place the steel trap is about the only trap that can be used; there being no timber over large portions of the Northwest and Canada.

I wait till ice is frozen over the runways and ponds, then I go at it making a circuit of the runways. I find where the mink go out from the shore to some muskrat's home, which will have a pole in it above water. I set two traps there, then look around. Close by I will find a small dump of trash made by muskrats, where the mink go to dung. I set two or three traps so when set and covered with fine brush they will be even with the surface and looking natural. I will then go on shore which is generally flat, following the mink signs I will find where they have dug into an old muskrat run. I put two or three traps around here close together so when caught the mink soon gets in two traps, then he is there to stay.

I use no bait when setting at a place like
this; the first mink caught smells the place up
so there is no need of any patent scent. Every
mink that gets on that swamp, if it is not over
two or three miles long, will visit that place in
one or two nights. At a place like that I leave
the traps all winter and will catch as many mink
as a trapper that scatters twice as many traps,
one in a place, all over the swamp.

There are one or two places in every swamp
or pond where nearly every mink will visit. It
may be a hole in a bank or an old muskrat house.
You can tell it by the signs or by tracks in the
snow. There is the place, then you are sure of
your mink.

I make small iron stakes to fasten my traps
where I can get nothing for a drag. I make
them myself. Take a rod $\frac{1}{4}$ inch thick, cut in
lengths 8 inches long, turn one end when hot
over the ring of trap chain, sharpen the other
end. I only lost one mink last winter by gnawing his foot off. A fish is good bait for mink,
also fish oil and fresh rabbits or birds. When
buying traps, buy the best, they are the cheapest
in the long run.

Some trappers buy the cheap traps and lose
enough fur the first season to pay for good traps.

I find that it pays to stretch and care for furs
well. I have bought furs that were not worth

one third price. Mink were stretched 6 inches wide at tail tapering to a point at nose, being 8 inches long, when they should have been 16 or 20 inches and 3 to 4 wide. Again I have got

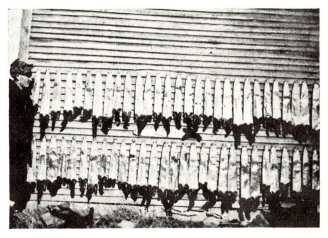

NICELY HANDLED MINK PELTS.

them that they were stretched so tight you could see through them.

Some trappers claim the mink is very sly and hard to trap, others that he is very easy to trap, and that they could catch an unlimited number if the mink were only plentiful in their locality. I always like to read anything I can find on this subject, says an Illinois trapper. Sometimes I find methods that I have used with good success, methods that I think would be good, and methods that I think would never work in any locality. Not like the muskrat, the habits of the mink are almost the same in all localities, but changing some in different seasons of the year. In Central Illinois along with the change of seasons, we have wet and dry seasons, and good methods of trapping in the dry season will not work at all in the wet.

When I first started trapping mink I met with very good success, not due to any good method, but as far back as I can remember I have always been a lover of nature, and I was not a stranger to the habits of the mink. And I will say right here to all young trappers, and also to some older ones—learn the habits of the animal you wish to trap, and if you are half a trapper, success will be yours. I have learned many things that I never knew before I trapped him, but I would not trade what I knew before for what I have learned since. I am going to try to make plain to you, brother trappers, some of the methods we use here in Illinois, and I believe these same methods will work in all localities.

This section of the country is cut up with small ditches and small creeks, ideal places for mink and muskrat. In the dry season all the tile ditches and small creeks have very little water in them, and no better places can the mink find than a dry tile or an old muskrat den. Here they will ve until the water drives them out in the spri

When setting the trap at a tile, if the tile is too large, a couple of sticks stuck in front of the tile will narrow the opening, and a trap set properly in front of the tile will be very apt to catch the mink going in or out of the tile. Always see that the jaws of the trap rest firmly on the ground and that there is no danger of dirt or sticks or even grass getting in between the jaws of the trap, for if it does you will lose your mink even if he gets caught. A mink that has once been caught in a trap is doubly hard to catch, although I have met two exceptions to that rule, and will say that they were two of the blindest mink I ever trapped.

Fine grass, dried willow leaves, rabbit fur, or most any light material that will not interfere with the workings of the trap and will not make too great a contrast to the surroundings, will be good to cover the trap. Always be careful not to disturb the surroundings too much, as a mink will notice this quicker than the scent you leave on the traps when you set them.

A good rule to follow is—always set your

trap facing the way you think the mink is going to come, never sideways if possible to set any other. In setting at an old rat den, if possible always set the trap a couple of inches inside of the den and pull the spring around so a mink going into the hole will not step on the spring.

If you catch a female mink first, always reset the trap, as the chances are greatly in your favor of catching the male soon, and if mink are plentiful in your locality you may catch as many as a half a dozen males if in the running season. If you can find where an old rat hole leads down to the edge of the water from the top of the bank, a trap set in the lower end of his hole will catch nearly every mink that comes along. They very seldom miss the chance to explore a hole of that kind. The old trapper that told me about this set said that he caught twelve mink in one season at a place of this kind, and all in the same trap, a No. 1 Newhouse. It had been a wet season this year I speak of, and I will tell you how I trapped mink in January and with six inches of snow on the ground.

The ditches and creeks all had water in them and were either frozen over or covered with drifted snow. My best set was to set a couple of traps in the warm water that came out of the tiles. A mink is a great lover of water and will play in a place of this kind for half an hour at a time, and two traps will almost catch him. Whenever there is a small air hole in the ice he will investigate, and if you place the trap directly under this hole he cannot very well miss getting caught. For this set the water should not be over four inches deep.

After the mink makes a hole through the snow drift he will always follow the same hole, will come into and go out of the water at certain places, and a trap set at any of these places is almost sure to catch.

As a scent bait, I use the matrix of the female mink taken in the running season, and for fresh meat bait I use rat, but I prefer the blind and water sets, and do not use the others until these two have failed only in the latter part of February and March. With slight changes I believe these sets can be used in most localities.

My experience in trapping is limited to one season, the last, during which I trapped 39 mink, besides the five that left their legs in traps and four taken by thieves and dogs. But my success has been so much above that of others who have tried to duplicate my luck, that I want to give some pointers to some who have not had satisfactory results in trapping mink, says a South Dakota party.

This is a well settled prairie country, with

5

one small creek running through it, and an occasional slough. Game of all kind is pretty well cleaned out. In fact, it was not generally known that any number of mink existed here. Being quite a hunter with nothing to hunt, I conceived the idea to trap a mink, and before I got through I found the sport more enjoyable and profitable than hunting. I had no trappers guide to help me, and it took me three weeks and more than a dozen trips to my traps to catch the first mink. But during that time my experience and observations were teaching me fast. And later when I saw a trap at about every hole in the country with seldom a catch, it amused me.

My receipt to a beginner is—get three sizes of traps, No. 0 to set at holes, No. 1 to set in water or path, and Stop Thief to set over holes that the others cannot be used at, or for sure catch when you know mink to be in. See that your traps have strong springs, and that when set fine the pan is on a level with jaws. All traps should be alike in this respect. Now to prevent them from rusting as well as to take the scent off, heat them enough to run some wax over them.

As to where to set them, you must find some signs of mink near water, tracks in sand, droppings, or best of all, used holes. Now remember you have to deal with some of the most intelligent but superstitious and shy of animals. I kept one at my house for a while and found him more intelligent than a cat or dog. They get bold and careless some times, but not very often. Their holes are frequently shallow, and they are suspicious of one's presence. The less you frequent the place and tramp about his paths, the better. Avoid the hole if possible.

First choice is to set the trap in shallow water on his runways, sticking up weeds if necessary to make him go over the traps. The next choice is where he goes in and out of the water. Next in dry path and last at his hole where he is the most suspicious of disturbance. Water set is the best and easiest, but even then the trap should be covered with light mud.

On dry land you should leave the place looking as natural as before. At the hole use a small trap, Blake & Lamb is the easiest and quickest set. Remove enough dirt to sink the trap to a level. Set trap with jaws never crosswise to the hole. Have jaws rest so that jaws will not tilt if stepped on. Now see that pan is set just about right, not too easy, and now you are ready for the most important part — to cover — so it will stay covered and spring regardless of freezing, thawing, snowing, or blowing, and not to clog the jaws with rubbish. It is too tedious to get the mink over the trap to have something go wrong at the critical moment. I use brown tissue paper or the fuzz from cattails, which I sprinkle with a little fine dirt or rubbish at hand, the chain having been previously staked and hid. All should now be left looking as natural as before, and one's tracks obliterated.

A well set trap will not reveal itself to the game or to any other trapper. A hole set trap should not be approached unnecessarily. Mink will seldom get in the first night, and it takes too long to reset them.

Mink will stay in holes several days if they fear danger. I had one stay twelve days because there was a Stop Thief trap over the hole, but I kept it there because there was a steam visible at the mouth of the hole, and I got her. I have used scent to some advantage, not to draw but to detract the mink's attention, but as to baits I have faithfully tried them all from muskrat to a frog, and I have never known a mink to approach any of them no matter where, when, or how left, except if left by themselves.

In the fore part of the winter I caught about all the males, perhaps because they were bolder. Later I got the females. The largest mink I got stretched 42 inches from tip to tip, and his hide on a five inch board was 24 inches. He was light brown. No. 0 held him by two toes. In fact, I never lost a mink from that sized trap. Those that chewed out were caught up too high.

My experience in trapping is altogether in mink and in a prairie country, and it has always been a great pleasure and very profitable for me, says an Iowa trapper. As I have said, trapping mink is a science which few trappers understand, and can learn only by long experience and

MOSES BONE.

close study. Any one taking two or three dozen traps and stringing them out, setting in holes and ditches, can catch a few mink. I know men who have trapped for years and claim to catch lots of fur, but it makes me smile to see how they set them; they simply don't know their A B C's about trapping mink.

The time that I have put in trapping mink for the last 37 years has paid me bigger money than anything I ever tried; of course I mean buying and shipping at the same time of trap-

ping. Counting ten hours as a day's work, I
have cleared from five to twenty dollars per day.
Now as I said several years ago, I have no secret
or I would let brother trappers have it; I use no
scent whatever but fresh bait, which is all that
is necessary.

You must learn by experience where and how
to set your trap. That is all the secret any mink
trapper has. The method for setting for mink,
rats or coon are all the same, can catch either in
the same trap. Water set is my way of setting
and far better than any other I think. In ditches
or streams where the water is shallow enough
to set your traps in where the current runs
against the bank; then scoop out a hole 8 inches
into the bank. I have used a butcher knife to
dig the mud out with; the water must flow into
the hole, which should be two inches deep. Cut
a forked stick, one prong one inch long, the other
6 or 8 inches long; sharpen it, run your bait on
this, put the stick in the back of the hole which
fastens your bait.

Now set your trap, turn the spring to one
side, fasten the chain the handiest way you can
so it is secure. I never had a mink cut his leg
off and get away. Now stick up weeds or sticks
on either side of the hole so the mink can't get
the bait without stepping on the pan of the trap.
The current should run strongly over the trap

so as to keep the water from freezing, for there are very few nights after trapping time sets in but that the water freezes in still water. I sometimes dam the water to make it run strongly over the trap. Everything about the trap should be left looking as natural as possible.

In cold weather I go on the same principle. When everything is frozen solid I use a hatchet cutting a hole in the bank; use ice or chunks of wood to make a lane to set your trap in, and throw your bait in as far as you can get it. Of course you cannot fasten it.

To show how well animals can scent a bait or anything of that kind I will relate an incident that happened several years ago. There was a fresh fall of snow and being warm the skunk were out of their burrows, and I was tracking one going southeast course. All at once it turned square to the left going some thirty feet and came to an old dried up mole covered with the snow. He nosed around it a while and then went the same direction as before. That showed plainly that animals can scent their game.

CHAPTER IX.

SOUTHERN METHODS.

On reading the methods used by the Northern mink trapper one is almost forced to the conclusion that the mink there is a different one from those here, (in Texas), but of course such is not the case. My limited experience in trapping mink here has brought me to the conclusion that they are not afraid of human scent, or old musty traps either. My opinion is that it is the disturbed surroundings that cause them to shy from the trap.

I once set a trap in a mink run in rather rank grass at 6 P. M. and the next morning had a No. 1 mink in it (poor color or course). The trap was not baited or scented and was set without gloves. Of course I did not tread down or pull up the grass to make a nice place to set, but stood at the side and slipped it in the trail in a slight depression. The mink did not seem trap shy although he had lost a foot in a previous experience.

There are any number of mink here, but the catch is rather small compared to the catch of other furs. I very often ask the trappers, "why

don't you go after mink, they will pay you best?"
The answer is invariably, "I can't catch them, I
don't know how." "Why don't you set your
traps in their runs, or at the mouth of the dens?"
Acting on this advice he sails out, finds a den,
leaves all his traps and other plunder at it, and
hikes out home for a spade and old Towser. They
both put in half a day, then give it up. Mr.
Mink is not at home. Can't trap them no how.
Sometimes he accidentally gets one. Then he
goes after them right, tears and digs up every
den he can find until his enthusiasm plays out.
By this time he has spoiled all, or a good portion
of his trapping ground, when if he had placed a
trap at the mouth of each den, and done it in a
proper manner, he might have caught twenty or
twenty-five mink during the season.

Now and then you find a fellow who has a
good mink dog and catches $75 or $100 worth of
them in a season. While this is all right for the
fellow that owns a dog, it does not fill my ideas
of getting mink pelts, as tearing and digging out
their dens has a tendency to cause them to hunt
homes elsewhere. I have caught four nice mink
at the mouth of one den in a single season, and
very likely I shall catch some there this season.
I do not cover the trap, nor do I use scent or
bait. I place the trap in a depression about four
or six inches from the mouth of the den; don't

cock the trap up so that he can see it twenty feet before he reaches it; arrange matters so he will have to get over the trap to get in the den. When he comes next time you will likely get him.

Mink here use the prairies around ponds and

A YOUNG TRAPPER.

small streams that drain the prairies. Around rice farms is a splendid place for them. They den in rank grass and sand knolls, and travel at night, in all kinds of weather, and very often you see them of foggy mornings. They feed on frogs, small fish, crawfish, birds, rabbits and the like, and very often they visit the poultry yards. My advice to the Southern mink trapper is, find where mink use, follow out their trails and runs. By noticing these closely you will find the places where he is compelled to put his feet or quit the trail. Here is the place to set your trap. Take a No. 1 of any good make, set it and adjust it properly and slip it in the trail through the grass, and be sure that the top of the jaws and spring are level with the ground. Do this in order that he can't see the trap until he is at, or in it.

In catching mink on the branches I very often use baits. When you find a log crossing the stream, cut a notch for your trap, and smear it with mud so it won't look fresh. It is the same with logs laying up and down streams. On these sets I use bait and a slight covering of fine trashy leaves. Put the bait under the trap, stake the chain to the side of the log, then place on the slight covering.

In most sets in winter I make them blind, but should surroundings require it, I bait. While I use a very small amount, I am not averse to using bait where I consider it required, and can say the same of covering for traps. As for scent, have never used any, but am of the opinion it would be of great help at certain seasons.

Mink is about all there is to trap in this part of North Carolina, and I have studied out a good many things about trapping them. I live where the country is hilly and has a good many branches and creeks, yet it is so thickly settled that mink are scarce. Up to within a year ago there was scarcely any trapping done about here.

Everybody seems to have a spite against the little mink, and whenever the dogs start one everybody lays aside everything to help kill the pesky varmint, and whoever kills it demands a chicken pie, whether he gets it or not. And for just such reasons as this they are very scarce, and it is very seldom that I can find the track of a real large one. I think they must get out of this neighborhood as soon as they are grown.

I have to conceal my traps very cautiously to catch these small and medium mink. When I am looking for a place to set my trap I select a narrow sand bar where they wade down into the water. I then dig out a place for the trap so it will set level and under water about a quarter of an inch; I then take some large water soaked leaves and cover the trap, then cover leaves with fine dirt or sand like that around trap. If the water is perfectly still, and nothing to bother covering, I prefer a piece of wet paper, a little larger than trap, instead of leaves.

I will say to those trappers who never use anything but leaves to cover their traps, that they could not get many mink around here that way, for I have tried it, and they would either go around trap or jump over it. Always carry some kind of firearms; it will more than pay for its trouble. Then too, it leads others to believe you are hunting and they won't be so apt to see you setting traps, and if you let as few as possible see you set traps you won't have to accuse "Sneakum" so often. It doesn't matter what you are trapping, cover your traps the best you can, and then it won't be a fine job; don't leave any loose dirt, tracks or anything else around trap that looks odd or unnatural; when you get your pelt, don't tear it off any old way, take your time and you'll get big pay for it.

In the following words I not only express my sentiments but the views of all trappers I have conversed with on the subject, writes a Texas trapper. Our mink are not at all educated. They are easily caught in traps not even concealed. The mink, as we all know, is fond of having food at all times, and when hungry does not appear to consider the trap an impediment.

Many are caught in Stop Thief Traps in this community. I was the first to introduce that trap in this section, and it has met with favor

because it deprives the mink of the privilege of
gnawing off his foot or leg. They are trapped
both in water and on land.

I have always had better success trapping
mink than other animals, often catching them by
their tails, which, by the way, is the best kind of
hold. If the mink here were trap-shy it would
be better for them, for there are very few of
them that have not met the trapper's fate.

A Southern trapper writes as follows: When
I was about fourteen years old I got hold of a
price list of raw furs and a kind of trapping
fever got hold of me and I purchased a trapper's
guide, and when I had studied it my father and
I set to work to make some traps. When we got
them done I went down to the branch near here
and set them the best I knew how for mink. I
tried him every way but never got a smell. So
I tried a year without success. Then I gave it
up for several years and thought I would have
to content myself working in the shop, as I am
a mechanic by trade and not a trapper.

In later years I thought I would try it again
as the mink were giving the poultry around here
trouble. So I set out again, and in the meantime
I received a price list and I noticed they adver-
tised animal bait for sale. I ordered a bottle of
mink bait and thought I would catch them.

When I received the bait I found where an old
mink or two had a runway in a small branch.
They would come up the branch every night. I

LARGE SOUTHERN MINK.

killed some birds and used some mink bait on
them and hung them over my traps. One old
dog mink would come within six inches of the

bait and my traps and did not pay any attention to it. I had some of my traps in water and some on sand bars concealed the best I knew how, but I did not get him that way.

One evening I was at the shop and I told my father I was going down to place my traps and see which was the smartest, the mink or me. I had noticed he would go by my traps and climb up a little bank and jump down over a root, so I set the trap there and covered with leaves. I had four traps set close together, and when I went to the sets the next morning I found him with a foot in each. He didn't dig and gnaw everything in reach as he was too badly tied up.

I thought I would get them all now, but I never got any more till last season. I wrote to the Oneida Community for a price list of traps and they mailed me one, and sent an advertisement of the F-F-G. So I subscribed at once and received the October number. In reading the letters I saw Brother F. M. Frazier's letter headed, "Advice to Young Trappers." I was impressed with the old gentleman's tone of writing so I wrote to him and asked him for help, and explained my difficulties to him. He gave me some fine sets and told me things I never thought of or heard of before, although I have since learned that they had been published in the F-F-G.

I purchased about thirty-nine second hand traps Nos. 1 and 1½. December 30th found me setting traps for mink. I carried out Brother Frazier's plans and directions. I made thirteen blind sets, and on Monday morning went around to see if anything was doing. The first trap I came to was sprung and had a mink's toe in it. I felt pretty bad, but that was more than I had gotten in a good while. So I went to another trap, and before I got there I saw everything gnawed up, and on going closer up jumped an old mink on a log near the trap. His eyes sparked but I soon put an end to him, and I have been catching mink ever since.

On February 1st I moved some of my traps down a river near here. I made most of my sets in water and used rabbit for bait. I made enclosures and put bait in back end of same and the trap at the entrance. I noticed a hole near the creek that emptied into the river and I set a trap at the hole. I have noticed that hole for several years and had been seeing a large mink on that creek for eight or ten years. I have seen his track where he would go in that hole every time he would go along by it, but when I set my traps there I didn't see any tracks. The next time I went there I found a large brown mink in my trap, but it wasn't the "big one."

I didn't get any more there for some time,

6

neither had I seen the big mink track since I set
my traps down there, but on going to my traps
one morning I saw that something was doing.
When I came close I saw that there was something big in the trap and had dragged the trap
back in the hole the full length of the chain. I
took hold of the chain and began to pull. I soon
pulled him out as far as his hind legs and he
looked so big I let go the chain and he went back
in the hole. I pulled him out and put a 22 between his eyes and that settled him. He measured thirty-two and a half inches from tip to tip
on the board. How is this for a large mink,
brother trappers?

CHAPTER X.

As for sets, I think it all depends upon the country and seasons. For mink in my country, Ontario, I prefer a hollow tree turned up at the roots, setting a No. 1 trap, baited with either fish or muskrat. Such a set should be on the bank of a lake or river, as a hungry mink going along the shore is always running in such old roots and logs. As for water sets, they keep freezing up, and another thing, it is not natural for a piece of meat to be hanging on a string.

A Michigan trapper writes as follows: Now brother trappers, are you energetically putting in your leisure time during September and October looking up new grounds for hunting and trapping and finding signs and trails of coon, mink and fox, or are you lounging around and putting all this off till it is time to take out your line of traps?

September and October is the time to ascertain where the game is, and if you wish success and good sport and increased revenue, it is to your interest to do a little hustling and by, watching their moves in your neighborhood. I

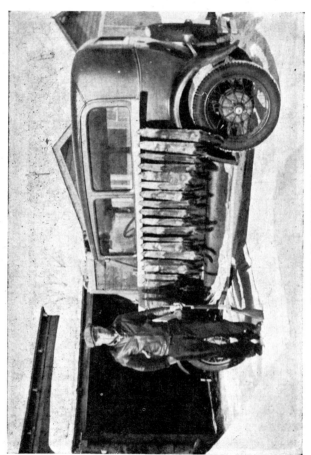

CAUGHT IN MINNESOTA.

have made mink trapping a specialty and for twenty-five years I have been successful in trapping him, and it did not take me long to appreciate one point, that is, I was up against a little animal of almost human intelligence, and to-day this animal is as smart and as shy as they ever were.

There are three rules very essential in trapping any kind of animals, one of the secrets of success is to know how, where and when to set a trap. Another is to get a dependable trap, which in my estimation is a Newhouse No. 1 and No. 2. I use these traps for every purpose from a weasel to a large coon. The third one I never vary from, and that is to set every trap as carefully as possible, as though it was intended to catch a shy mink or coon, as one of these animals will often happen around when one least expects it.

It is best to set a trap in good shape and always take time and conceal each trap carefully. I have before now set traps all around in wood and field for skunk. I have gone the rounds to my skunk traps and found a fine big coon or weasle instead of a skunk, or to my rat traps and found a large mink or raccoon instead of a rat, and these lucky surprises occurred because my traps were well set and concealed.

I will not outline my method how to set, but you may bet your old hat you will take Mr. Coon or Mink, or whatever animal happens along in your neighborhood, and you know where their trails are. From October until trapping time look for their signs and tracks along water edge, in woods, in old roads, cow paths in woods, pastures and fields, and under fences, keeping all these places in mind until the time for trapping comes. Then take with you lots of traps, then you know where to set.

Smoke your traps before setting, handle everything with gloves on, cultivate the habit of leaving the place with as little change as possible, and finish the job by brushing away your tracks immediately around the traps. Then visit your traps regularly and without any unnecessary company.

Trappers often notice that fur bearing animals have disappeared from the localities where once they were numerous. There are many reasons for this disappearance, the destruction of their dens or trees in which they live. No true trapper will cut a coon tree or dig out dens of mink, skunk or fox, if he wishes to ever trap on the same ground again.

Now I am not a professional trapper, says a Minnesota trapper, but I make all animal habits a very close study, and love to be among them in their wild homes and love to set a trap once in a while just for experience, and never fail to get my game.

The other day I went rabbit hunting. We have about two inches of fresh snow. I got one rabbit and found a fresh mink track so I concluded to follow him. Inside of a hundred yards I found another hole where he came out dragging something. I still followed. Another fifty yards further I found where he went in another hole (it was in a bog) and found a muskrat half eaten up and a fine place to set two traps.

I had no traps with me, so I marched home about four miles and got two traps all rusted up and tied with a piece of copper wire. I greased them up with sewing machine oil and started back. When I got to the place it was getting dark and I had to set the traps by match light.

I will tell you how I set the traps to fool the mink so he could not smell the traps or machine oil. I took the muskrat and rubbed all over the traps with the bloody side and set the traps one in each hole, and took an oak leaf and smeared blood on and laid it on the pan of each trap, and then laid the muskrat in the center of the two so he would have to cross either trap to get the rat. I then covered the hole up with the same dirt and moss that I dug out, and went home. At five o'clock the next morning I left home to get my prize.

I got there by daylight and there was Mr.
Mink caught in both traps, one on each foot. He
was the largest mink I got that winter. He was
brown and when stretched measured exactly
thirty-five inches from tip to tip.

I almost always trap mink in the winter with
blind sets, says a Wisconsin trapper, by chopping a place for the trap so it will be, when set,
about level with the surface of the mink's trail
in front of the holes that the mink makes in the
snow. I then take cat tails that grow in the
marshes and spread some on trap bed; I then
place my trap and next some more cat tails
spread on top of traps, and last some snow which
I spread over it all with a twig carefully so it
will be nice and smooth. The cat tail I spread
under the trap is to keep the trap from freezing
fast at the bottom. I have had very good success
with this set. I used bait altogether, but very
few mink can now be caught around here with
bait.

I once set a trap for a mink alongside of a
log which lay across the stream, setting the trap
on the shore near the ice while standing on the
log; there was about 20 inches of snow on the
ground, so it left a space behind the trap in
which I placed a piece of rabbit. The next morning I should have had a mink but instead of that

the mink had that piece of rabbit, and a larger hole alongside the log showed that it had been dragged further back under the snow. I then set my trap again, tying fast another piece of rabbit, but Mr. Mink had enough rabbit for a while, so about five days afterwards I had a squirrel in it.

I then threw the rabbit away and put the squirrel in the snow along the side and above the trap, with only the tail out of the snow. About three days more and something had happened. The trap laid sprung in the place I had set it and in it was the tip of a squirrel's tail, and the squirred I had laid for bait was gone. This might seem untrue but it is only too true, although just how it might have happened I cannot account for.

I then kicked up the snow and found that the mink had come from under the ice on the other side of the log and circled the end of the log, coming in behind the trap after the bait, all the way traveling under the snow. I have never gotten that mink, but have learned better ways since that time, and find that where mink are trapped much the blind set is by far the best.

CHAPTER XI.

UNUSUAL WAYS.

We can hardly approve of some of the methods herein described, but they will doubtless continue to be employed so long as they are not prohibited by law. Occasionally too, there might be circumstances to justify resorting to the most objectionable of them, writes a trapper and hunter of Maine.

The first of those I will speak of requires a good dog, one that will follow the mink's track and drive him to hole. Nearly any intelligent dog, with a fair amount of the hunting instinct can soon be trained to do this by allowing him to smell a few mink carcasses while skinning, and calling his attention at every opportunity to the trails of the animals along the streams, following them up and making an effort to bag the mink, with his help, as often as possible. The first snows afford good conditions for the rudimentary training, as the trail can then be plainly seen by the trapper (or rather hunter as he should be styled in this case) while a good scent is left for the dog.

Having qualified the dog for tracking, the

next requisite is a partner. This, of course, means a division of the profits, but it is unavoidable, as the work cannot be performed satisfactory by one alone. Indeed, it will more often be found convenient to have yet a third hand, which may be a boy to manage the dog and assist generally.

A FEW GOOD ONES.

A meadow brook, not too large, with low, spongy banks, can be worked to best advantage. Look the ground well over in advance, acquainting yourself with the haunts of the game, and all the holes and other places in which a mink is likely to take refuge when pursued. For an outfit you need at least a crowbar and shovel (some-

times a sharp pointed, hardwood stick can be
made to answer for the former) and each man
should have a gun.

Go to the brook in the early morning, before
the scent has had time to cool. Allow the dog to
hunt along the borders and under the banks and
when he picks up a track, work along with him
until he has the game in hiding. You will find it
necessary to assist him considerably, as mink by
no means always travel on land. When one
takes to the water, as they usually do at short
intervals, the trail is broken beyond the ability
of the strongest nosed dog to follow at such
times as this, that is when Mr. Mink takes the
brook for it, one should go ahead with the dog
and find where he resumed dry footing. It will
probably not be far, for he is in and out every
few yards or so, and if you go far without striking the trail you had better turn back, for he is
most likely hiding in the bank somewhere behind you.

After locating the hole where he is hiding, let
the dog dig him out while a man stands a little
distance up and down the brook respectively,
with gun ready cocked for him when he comes
along. If the hole extends some distance back
into the bank, the rear end may usually be
reached, after a few trials, by thrusting the bar
down from overhead, which will have the effect

to send the hunted animal forth in a hurry. Often, however, the spade will have to be brought into requisition and used freely before the object is accomplished.

At first he will probably forsake one hole only to take refuge in another, but when he finds that you are really after him, and that there is, moreover, a dog in the racket, he will try the dodge of swimming under water. Then is your time. Watch for him at the shallow places, where he will prove an easy mark. Have guns loaded light and aim to have charge strike a little to one side of body. The concussion will be sufficient to stop him, and the fur will not be injured as in firing point blank. It is exciting sport for the mink is like "greased lightning" in his movements, and if given the least chance will outwit both dog and man and escape.

An old New Hampshire gunner told us that he and his partner once got sixteen mink this way in one week, the best of which brought them twelve to fifteen dollars a skin. He knew absolutely nothing about trapping so resorted to this method instead. We have mentioned spade, bar and guns as comprising the necessary outfit, but of course various other implements of one's own invention and manufacture can often be used to advantage. Some make great account of a piece of wire with a sharp hook at one end for thrust-

ing into the hole and drawing the mink to the
light, as a trout from the water. Others use a
long handled spear to thrust under banks, or to
pinion the game when going through shallows.
A truly barbarous practice besides the further
objections of greatly damaging the pelt of the
animals taken thus.

Another mode of capturing the mink is to
lie about the streams on wet and foggy days and
shoot him. They travel a great deal in such
weather. By selecting a spot where you can keep
well hidden, yet commanding a long stretch of
beach under some overhanging bank, you stand
a good chance to secure a shot if you have plenty
of patience. Of course you would not be apt to
get many in a day, but one mink represents a
pretty good day's work at the price they are sell-
'ng now.

One characteristic of the animal should be
borne in mind when pursuing this method of
hunting him, and that is his persistency in going
whichever way he wishes to go. If a mink starts
to go up a brook he's going up before he gets
through with it, or lose his life trying; and down
the same. The more anybody or anything tries
to prevent him, the more desperate and reckless
he grows in his efforts to accomplish his aim. So
if one sees you and turns back startled don't follow him, but just crouch down in a convenient

hiding place and wait for him.   The chances are
ninety to one that he will soon be back again.

I have known trappers to have good success
taking mink with a common box trap such as is
used in catching rats about the house and barn,
and I am inclined to think that aside from its
bulkiness this is a pretty good sort of trap. Some
use poison as for the wolf, but the use of this on
animals was always repugnant to me.

Perhaps the queerest method of which I ever
heard was that mentioned by a gentleman in
Illinois. He claimed to have caught mink with
an ordinary fish hook, baited, and attached to a
piece of wire.

I do not believe, however, that any of the
methods mentioned in this article are equal for
effectiveness and true sport to the regular way
with steel trap or deadfall. Some af them, it
seems to me, I could not be induced to make use
of on any account. And yet, as already stated,
one might find himself in circumstances that
would justify their adoption.

CHAPTER XII.

I for one will say that the mink is a very shy animal, but I do claim he can be caught if you study him and set your trap in the right place. I will suppose that you are trapping along a small stream. All you need is plenty of traps, a belt with a small hatchet attached, a small caliber pistol, and a pair of hip rubber boots. A pair of these boots are as necessary in a trapper's outfit as the main spring is in the watch or clock. Be sure to have your traps in good working order.

Oh yes, I forgot the scent. This you can make yourself by cutting up a couple of cats and musk-rats in fine pieces and let them rot good, then add some fish oil and four or five different kinds of oil that you can buy at a drug store. To make this scent all the better you had better put in about one-half pound of limburger cheese. Now then you got her to smelling just right, and every mink that gets a whiff of this perfume will say, oh joy, and hike off in the other direction as fast as his legs can carry him. I took a little bottle of this great scent with me once on a trapping trip. I carried it in my coat pocket.

I was leaning over some roots setting a trap
when the cork came out of the bottle — well, you
know the rest. I never need to hunt for this
coat when I want to put it on, for it always
makes itself known.

You are now ready to set your traps. You
might take a couple of dogs and several small
boys to help track up the ground. This the mink
can see and smell, and it makes him easier to
catch. Now then when your traps are on your
back, get down into the water, and be careful
when going in and out of the water and make
tracks in mud and on side of bank.

The place to set your trap is on the edge of
the water. Walk along in the water and examine every hole just even with the water's
edge. Some of the holes may come out several
inches under water. Set your trap here in water
2½ inches deep, turn spring to right and cover
trap with a muddy leaf, fasten trap with a stick
run through ring, and have chain stretched out
in deep water as far as it will reach. You will
see that you haven't touched a thing but your
trap and stake. As for the trap, the running
water will clean it of any scent you may have
left on by handling, but the stake I splash with
water and wash a little. If in setting the trap
you touch or step on the bank, wash out your
tracks with water.

Now then move on, and if you come to a tree on the bank that has lots of roots just even with the water, examine it close, for here is a good place for a mink den. If you find a hole set your trap as before, being careful to leave things as they were. A place where the bank guides the mink into the water is a good set. If you set a trap and have reason to think that the mink will walk around it, then stick up small sticks and little bushes so as to make a fence to guide your mink into the trap. A mink is not afraid of it, for he sees bushes in the water, and it will not scare him a bit.

The way just spoken of, of sticking sticks across the water, is a very important way to catch mink, and advise all trappers to give it a little more thought. If you trap along a ditch or a very small stream just try it. Stick your sticks across the stream just like a little fence, leaving three gaps, one at each end and one in the middle. Set your three traps here, and I bet you will get nearly every mink that goes up that stream. Of course, stand in the water while you are doing all of this, and your success will be doubly better.

When you put out a line of traps where there are mink, hide every trap as carefully as you can. Suppose you set a trap uncovered at what you suppose to be a muskrat hole, you don't know

TRAPPING DOWN STREAM.

but what some mink might come along, and on entering the hole he sees the trap—well, it don't take him long to leave the place.   Then boys, the very next hole that mink goes into he will look for another trap.   You don't need to fool a mink very often until he becomes educated, and then catch him if you can.

To catch mink successfully you must have open water.   I very seldom set for mink when water is all frozen up.   Did you ever notice that you made your best catch of mink on a snowy or rainy night?   Now, why is this?   It is because your tracks and scent were either washed out or covered up by snow.   A mink is not a hard animal to catch if you have water and weather just right, and you are careful about setting your trap.   But he is a very shy animal, and boys if you are not careful to study his habits you will pay dear for every pelt you get.

CHAPTER XIII.

EXPERIENCED TRAPPERS' WAYS.

At first when I started to trap I thought I could catch mink every time, says an Iowa trapper. That was three years ago this last February. Well I caught two mink that spring and seven the next winter and sixteen the next. That was the first season that I was able to catch every mink that trots or lopes my way, big, little, old and young are treated all alike; sometimes it takes a mink three or four days to come out of a hole when you track him in.

A water set is a pretty good set for mink but you cannot find many springs that you can set a trap in the winter time, so I set dry sets for them. At a hole is a good place. Put a piece of muskrat carcass in the hole to keep the rabbits from going in and set a Blake & Lamb trap in the entrance. Chop a hole in the frozen ground large enough for the trap and cover it with tissue paper and thinly with dry dirt. Be sure to put some dry material of some sort under the trap to keep it from freezing down, have the surface of the ground level after it is covered over with dry dirt so you cannot tell just exactly where the trap is yourself, or in other words don't have a high place where the trap is when it is covered over. Fasten the trap to a drag of some sort. If you fasten to something solid the mink will pull out if he is only caught by the toes.

I caught two mink one winter that only had three legs. They were the ones that pulled out of my traps because I had the trap fastened too solid. One mink I caught was only caught by one toe and was tied to a little brush drag; when I tracked him up I found that he had gone about ten rods. When I got in sight of him he got stout and pulled out and started off at a pretty stiff gait, and I had to let the dog catch him for he was geared up too high for me to catch.

Trappers, have you not had your mink trap set and baited under a shelving bank and seen mink tracks going up and down by the bait and they would not touch it? Get some sticks and stick them from bank down into water that is five or six inches deep, is the advice of a Maine trapper. Leave a place for trap up next to bank where he travels and cover nicely with fine rotten wood, and you will get more mink setting this way than you will with all the bait you bother with, that is, if you pick out such places along the brook and stick up sticks close enough so he cannot get by without going over trap.

EASTERN TRAPPER AND TRAPS.

I don't mean to say that bait isn't good, because I have caught a good many with bait, and there are lots of times when I can't find such a place and of course use bait and scent. Some say mink are afraid of human scent and set the trap with gloves, and that they are foxy and hard to catch. I don't think a mink knows any more than a skunk, and I can catch them just as easy. Last winter I went to my trap one morning and found two toes of a mink in one and one toe in another, and inside of a week I had both of them in the same trap and in the same place.

Mink are not very plentiful in some places which makes some people think they are hard to catch, and others don't know how to set a trap right for mink.

The first requisite in trapping mink is water, either a lake or river, says a Minnesota trapper. Small streams are to be preferred, and the swifter the current the better. Why? Because swiftly running water does not freeze so quickly, a fact every boy knows.

Next, select a spot on the shore where the bank is steep, ascending directly up from the water, and place your trap (a No. 1 or 1½ of any good make) in about two inches of water and about six inches from the bank, and fasten trap by driving a stake full length of chain out in the water.　Many trappers advocate the use of both bait and sliding pole or spring pole, but personally I do not care for either, unless there is danger of trap lifters "swiping" your game; in such cases the sliding pole is the best, as it is more humane and game is entirely concealed.　If the bank is not too high set your trap from the top and place in position with a stick, for by so doing you do not make any muss around the trap.

Now let me caution young trappers about setting too many traps for one mink.　One trap well set is better than a dozen just slung in or even well set and carefully concealed.　It is not necessary to have four or five traps within a radius of six feet as young trappers often do.　I discovered a case of this kind once.

For two weeks once I was after a sly representative of the mink family but without success.　Every trick in my command was tried without success, but one morning I determined to try for him up a small spring creek, where he was in the habit of going　I hesitated about putting my traps on this creek.　I had hesitated about putting my traps on this creek as the owner usually lifted all traps found there.　As there was no snow there except small patches I was not aware of another trapper's work on this brook, but a few drops of blood on a patch of snow caused me to open my eyes, and I was not long in discovering his traps. A blind man could have done that for they were literally thrown in, some almost upside down and others with the spring half out of the water.

I followed his line for about twenty rods, and then discovered the place of capture. Six traps were set in as many holdes, and all in a radius of five feet, but they had done the business. Was I mad? I shall leave it to the reader to guess. Boys, let me tell you this capture was an accident and not the result of skill.

I have endeavored to explain as simply as possible one set for mink, but this method will not answer all winter, for all the streams will freeze during extreme cold weather. On nearly all lakes and rivers springs can be found, and here is the place for your traps in cold weather. Common sense will show you the most suitable spot for the set. All minks have a weakness for wading in such springs, and a trap carefully placed and concealed will get a mink if there are any in the vicinity.

It was early in the fall of 1901 and I was working on the farm. I one day saw signs of mink under a bridge near home so I had a friend who was working for us set two traps for him that day, writes another party from Minnesota. I set the traps a few inches under water, covered them with wet leaves, thinking, "I will have you tomorrow." Well, the next morning we came along but no mink, so in the afternoon we looked at them again and Mr. Mink got in one trap, pulled it in between two logs, and the other trap was sprung. I then pulled on the other chain and the mink was in the trap. I pulled and all at once his foot slipped out. This taught Mr. Mink a lesson.

I set my traps again, and after this he sprung traps about as fast as I could reset them. So I set six more traps and got some ten and twelve inches under water. I used to reset the traps before I went to dinner, and after dinner he had every one sprung and the water looked very muddy. I laid for him but never did see him. I trapped for that mink every year until 1904. I saw his tracks on the snow so I got out some snow sets and one January morning I found him dead in the trap. He was a large dark mink and had lost all his toes by traps.

A good place to catch mink is at the mouth of a spring. Get your traps well under water and cover up with wet leaves, as a mink usually goes up such a small stream. I will say to the beginner, never get cheap traps, as they are the dearest in the end. Never catch fur until it is prime.

I find no difficulty in catching mink if they are plenty, but thin them down to one or two well educated animals and your task is different, says an Ohio trapper. Where plenty I set in riffles, building stone walls or staking across not too high, a foot is plenty, leaving one or more openings, according to width. Place a

BARRICADE SET.

trap (No. 1 or 1½ Newhouse is best) in each opening. I invariably stake at such places for it attached to chunks, bushes or small logs, the trap is liable to float away in sudden rising of high water. Place a trap at mouth of tiles, ditches or drains, staking well out from trap. I have caught a great many mink along where the over-hanging sod had curled down, leaving a

space between sod and bank sometimes of a good
length.   This is a capital place to catch mink, as
every one that goes up and down that side will
almost always go through.   All trappers know
mink are very inquisitive about such places, and
if the place is formed in summer or early fall
they will already have used it as a runway.
After finding such a place, put a trap at one or
both ends of hole.   Set trap level and cover well
but not too deep, and I am sure if there are any
mink traveling the stream you will stand a fair
show of getting them.   I have caught two mink
at such places, one in each trap in the same
night, more than once.

An old hollow log is also a good place for
mink with a trap at each end.   You will notice
when there is a light shift of snow that mink
cross old logs, limbs, boards and dams that are
across streams.   Put your trap in the center of
crossing place, as you cannot tell where he will
get on or off at.   Always cover traps when not
setting in water.   Old hollow stumps, trees,
openings in fences, stone walls, or flood-gates,
drifts and the like are good places to set traps
for mink; path openings in brush, in fact anywhere you see signs of their travels, as they most
generally have a route which they follow more
or less.   I have followed them across country
from the headwaters of one stream to another,

to swamp and swales where the muskrat abounds, turning every "hole inside out," so to speak, and they seem to know them all.

For bait I use fish oil, you can get it almost anywhere and it is cheap and good, the older the better. Place a few drops on the end of a tile, roots of a tree or stone, or in fact anywhere you have a trap but not on your trap. I never put it on dead bait but just sprinkle it around. A mink likes to kill his own game. Make him think there is some around and hunt for it, which he surely will do if there is nothing but the scent to find.

To be a successful mink trapper you must study his trails and set your trap accordingly.

Most methods that I read for trapping the mink are for trapping in the north or far north. Now some of them are good, while others are useless here. From my observation of the habits of the mink in Virginia, I don't think they have any fixed abode (in trapping season anyhow). Wherever is most convenient after a full meal or light overtakes them they den up for the day, and the next day may be snugly sleeping under the roots of a blown over tree or under the banks of a creek five miles away. The building of barricades of rocks, old chunks or pens of sticks and bait within is time and labor thrown away. Now, young trapper, I am going to give you four of my favorite sets for mink, that if you follow will give you some success, if there are any mink where you are trapping.

Follow along ditches and find where they cross, usually called secret ditches, which come into the main one, set your trap at the entrance of the covered one a little under water, and cover with water soaked leaves. Do not use bait but may use scent, or a decoy. One may be fixed by making a box about 6 inches square, 12 or 18 inches long, of old boards, with hoe plant in bank at desirable place so as to look natural. Set your trap in front.

Another is to get a piece of hollow log 3 or 4 feet long, place in mouth of ditch or branch where it comes into creek, anchor with stakes or weigh down with stones, close one end, place trap at other, under water if possible; place bait in log. This is a sure set for coon. It took me nearly half a day last September to cut a log, get in branch and weigh down with stones to keep high water from washing away, but caught four mink and two coon at the entrance.

Another is where banks are steep along small streams. Set trap in water, cause anything that may come along to pass over trap by a row of dead sticks, weeds or a bunch of old weeds. I have also caught many by placing two old logs five or six feet long, four or five inches apart in shallow water near a steep bank, cover with a larger log. If you have plenty of traps you can set one in each end. Do not use bait but can use scent. Be sure to search out all the old hollow logs near streams and set trap in or near entrance—place bait in log. By following these rules any one, where game is fairly plentiful, can catch some mink.

CHAPTER XIV.

MANY GOOD METHODS.

Last winter I knew of at least eight trappers who were trapping for mink along the same stream where I was trapping, and while all of them combined caught four mink, I had the good luck of catching thirteen in my traps and I shot one one morning, making fourteen in all, says an Ohio trapper.

I wonder how many readers have ever heard a mink scream when in a trap? I think it is the most blood-curdling hair-raising noise I have ever heard; it is equal to the scream of a panther. I had great sport last winter by sending some young boy trappers out to track a mink to his den. I told them that all they had to do was to follow him to the last hole he crawled into and then set their traps, but after following him for about three miles they came back discouraged and disappointed. They said he had gone into about one thousand holes, but had always come out again, and such was a fact.

I don't know how they do in other parts of the country, but here it is next to impossible to track one down; it looks as if they never stop. I have followed them for six miles already and they were still going on; I don't believe that they have any regular den or hole after the breeding season is over; you just have to catch them on the run.

One evening last fall I was sitting on the creek bank fishing when a very large mink came up the creek by me and he was a curiosity; his tail was just as white as snow. I tried awfully hard to get hold of him last winter, but failed. I presume he never stopped until he reached the north pole.

I have two methods for trapping them; one is to find a hole along some stream, an old musk-rat or woodchuck hole is best. If there are no holes it is an easy matter to make one. It is a well-known habit of the mink to be crawling into every hole he comes to, and I have known them to go one hundred yards out of their path, just for the pleasure of investigating an old woodchuck hole.

After finding a suitable hole for setting your trap, throw a piece of muskrat liberally doped with equal parts of oil of peppermint and sweet oil back in the hole, and set your trap at the entrance; use a little care in concealing the trap and sprinkle a few drops of the above oil over the trap, and you may be sure of having the pleasure of skinning the first mink that somes along.

I have caught them as far as two miles from
any stream in my coon and fox traps, so that
goes to prove that they do not stay along the
streams altogether.

Another method I use, and the one I consider
the best, is to go along the banks of some stream,
where you are sure that mink are in the habit of
traveling, then get four old boards, six or eight
feet long and six inches wide, (if necessary logs
can be used instead of boards) then stake them
down on their edges so that they will form the
letter X, only instead of crossing them leave a
small opening of three or four inches like this ✗
for the mink to run through, then set the trap a
few inches either way from the center, or two
traps can be set, one on each side of the center.
They will never jump over the boards, but instead they will guide them over the trap.

After an experience of 34 years in trapping
mink I presume I can give a few points, writes
Mr. Moses Bone, of Iowa, that may help younger
trappers who wish to trap mink. The mink is
very cunning and hard to catch in a steel trap
unless you know how and where to set, which is
about the only secret there is in catching mink.
I have had people write to know what scent I
used and how I set traps. A man can learn better methods as long as he traps — experience is

the best teacher — and unless he is willing to work hard he will never make a successful trapper of any kind of game. A trapper simply wants to shoulder his traps early in the morning and travel ten, twenty and perhaps thirty miles a day; he must foot it, for no other method of traveling will do. The writer has done it many times, starting before daylight and not getting home until after dark.

As before stated, my experience as a mink trapper began 34 years ago, my brother and I trapping together, and we began putting out our traps the first week in November, 1867. There were very few trappers then and mink were plentiful. In four weeks we caught 101 mink and 50 muskrats. The mink were mostly in prime condition and brought $300.00. Rats at this time were worth 25 cents each.

At the beginning of the trapping season my brother in one night caught 15 mink, the largest catch I ever knew. In 1873 I caught 10 mink in one night, but it took two days to visit my traps, walking 60 miles. In 1878 I caught 15 mink in one hole where the water ran all winter, and I never had to bait the trap as the scent was enough to attract every mink coming near. In the past three years I have caught 90 mink within a mile of home. Several years ago I caught 8 in one place.

I use steel traps, not so many as I used to, as
trappers are numerous nowadays.   Water set
was always my favorite way of catching mink,
setting about two inches under water, in a
spring, ditch or where the water ran swift, otherwise the water will freeze over.   Of course when
very cold weather comes, dry land sets must be
resorted to.   I always use No. 1 steel traps.   No.
$1\frac{1}{2}$ is better for skunk or coon.   For bait use
chicken, rabbit, or still better, muskrat, but they
must be strictly fresh.

In order to make mink trapping interesting
one must make it pay, and where there are
plenty of the animals the scientific trapper can
make it pay, for they are about as easily caught
as any other game when you understand your
business.   Mink fur is not good and prime before
the middle of November in Iowa and states in
same latitude, and it is useless to catch them
earlier.

When you see signs of the mink set your
trap as near as you can get to a spring, ditch or
running water with a steep bank a foot or more
high.   Here dig a hole in the bank 6 or 8 inches
inward and low enough to let the water flow in.
Now get a forked stick, cut off one fork say an
inch long, leaving the other 6 or 8 inches long.
Sharpen the end of the long fork and run it

through your bait (remember bait must be fresh) up to the fork. The bait is now fastened on the stick and run it in the bank back in the hole as far as you can.

If any mink comes along they will find it. Set your trap near entrance, but always in the current. Take weeds or sticks, say a foot long, stick them in the mud, making a lane so the mink must pass over the trap in order to get the bait.

If you wish a good scent to draw mink in the spring of the year, collect the scent bags of the muskrat and preserve them in alcohol, to which is added 5 cents worth of oil of cumin if you like. I discarded all scents, however, 30 years ago, finding nothing better than fresh bait, the more bloody the better. The mink has a good smeller. For dry land set I go on the same principles, but cover traps with leaves, grass or fine rubbish.

This method is very successful for mink, and in fact for almost any fur bearing animal that travels up and down a creek, says an Illinois trapper. The first thing to do is to set your trap near the shore so it will be about two inches under water. Stake the trap or fasten it to a drag, just as you like. The trap should be a No. 1½ or you can set two or three No. 1 traps to-

gether. Now after the trap is set, get some
weeds or brush and begin at the trap and make
a V shaped pen, leaving an opening where the
trap is about ten inches wide if you are trapping
for coon. The brush or weeds, whichever is

NORTHWEST TRAPPER AND MINK.

used, should extend several feet from the trap
in either direction.

After you are through it should be like illustration No. 1. This, we will suppose, is for catching animals coming down the creek. Now go
down the creek a few rods and set another trap,
but have the narrow opening of the pen pointing

up the creek, as in the illustration No. 2, which will catch an animal traveling up the creek. If these pens are made right, then a mink will walk into the pens and through the opening nine times out of ten instead of walking around them. Try this method once and be convinced. These pens should be about a foot high.

If brush is used it should be fine so it will lie close together so a mink cannot pass through. If there is danger of the creek washing the brush away, then fasten it by driving a few small stakes in the ground to hold it.

Remember that no bait or scent should be used. If footprints are left on the ground, then splash water on them. Remember that half of the pen is on the shore and the other half is in the creek, providing the creek is a wide one; this depends on the width of the creek. It is a good idea to trap on both sides of a creek; one is sure then of catching an animal whether it goes down on one side or the other. This is the only method I use and it has proven to be successful.

If a mink is hungry and finds bait that has been left for him he will pay no attention to human scent, while if he is not hungry he will not take the bait be it ever so fresh. A mink will sometimes make a trail in the fresh snow by passing several times over the same route and then never use that trail again. I have known otter to do the same.

I caught two mink last winter in a ditch, setting trap in the water. The first night I caught a medium sized mink and the third night I caught a small one, and would have caught every mink that went up that ditch if it had not frozen up and snowed so during the time that I could not keep the traps properly set.

If a person sets out a line of traps in this country, Iowa, while there is snow on the ground, he is simply going to a great deal of trouble to give them to some one.

In trapping mink I watch for signs, and when I locate a mink I consider it mine and it generally is, while if you bait up a trap somewhere that you may think is a good place to catch a mink, it often happens that you may make a good many trips to your trap before you get a mink, and you may say to yourself that it is human scent that keeps them away, when perhaps there has not been a mink near the trap. My advice to young trappers is not to set where a mink may go but set it where you know he is going, and you will find it no trick to catch mink.

I have many different ways of trapping the mink, says a Pennsylvania trapper, as I set my traps only where I see their signs, and as the signs are often different, and found in different kinds of places, one way is not enough. I use Blake & Lamb No. 1 traps mostly for mink. I never stake a trap down except in water set. On dry land I fasten to a brush clog.

If one sets only where he sees the signs, and only sets one or two traps for each mink, from one to two dozen traps are all that are required. In the fall and early winter I set my traps in natural enclosures in old drifts, in hollow logs, under roots of trees, etc., baiting with fresh muskrat, fish, rabbit, chicken, mice or birds, using fish oil or muskrat musk for scent.

I do not believe in using mixed scents. In late winter and early spring I set traps in the same kind of places but without bait, using the musk of mink for scent. The mink is not looking for food then, and such scents as fish oil and muskrat musk are not as good as the musk of the mink itself.

The traps should always be covered with some light substance, which will not look out of place. Never smoke your traps, boil them in walnut hulls, maple bark or sweet fern. Mink may also be caught by tying a rabbit in a chunk of a hollow log, blocking one end shut and setting his trap in the other end.

When streams are open the shyest mink may

be caught by putting several small live fish on a string and stretching the string in a V shaped enclosure, in shallow water, setting the trap at the open end. Mink are easily caught by setting the trap at the foot of a steep bank which they use. If the trap is properly set, the bank will guide the mink into the trap.

There are many other ways of trapping the mink, where the signs are different, and found in different places. An experienced trapper can trace a mink for miles, where another person would not see a sign. A trapper must be able to read signs as he would read a book. As to human scent, that is all nonsense. The scent will not hang to the trap or bait more than a couple of hours.

I find a stream where mink frequent, look for tracks either in or out of water, close to edge, however, says an Arkansas trapper. Now don't set your trap on a track thinking you will get a mink, but look for a slide; mink have a slide same as otter; don't set on slide but go above slide along the bank where water is not over four inches deep. Set a No. 1 or 1½ trap, cover spring, don't disturb bank but just lay a small pole, attach your trap chain to this, cover trap and chain with old wet leaves. Don't take your hands, get a stick and rake the leaves over it, and do not let any one cause you to think that mink are not afraid of human scent. Be sure to crowd your trap against bank as a mink travels close to the bank. This is one way.

Another is, find a tree that has the earth washed away from the roots to the water, it being right against the bank, look in the shallow water around roots for mink tracks, if any, set trap. Again crowd bank with trap and you may expect mink from under that tree.

Another way is in looking along the bank of stream you will notice small holes straight back in bank just under water, extending back perhaps 4 or 6 inches; a mink did it. Look a little further and you will see a hole extending back in bank. It may be 6 or 8 inches across, extending back from 4 to 8 inches. Every time a mink travels this stream he visits these holes. He dug them to get crabs and small fish to bed in them. He catches them on his rounds. Now set a trap at mouth of hole and you can get a mink.

I have used bait. When I do I prefer red bird or woodpecker. Fix your bait always so mink cannot get at it without crossing or getting over trap. I believe this is sufficient, however, an old trapper or an experienced one needs no pointers, he will get the game.

Two years ago last fall I had a line of traps consisting of a few fox traps and the rest mink

NORTHERN MINK TRAPPER'S SHANTY.

traps, about fifteen in all, says a Maine trapper.
My partner, Dan, was a very young trapper,
having caught only a few mink and skunk. I
would rather have trapped alone, but as I was
just starting in I thought I would rather have
some one with me that knew a little more about
it. So one November morning we started out
all aglow and pushed on by the cool morning air
we set the above named traps and returned
home very tired and weary, but the thought of
bringing back a fox or a nice mink the next day
gave me more life, and I retired happy enough
for my day's work.

The next morning we were up early and
made our rounds, but to our great disappoint-
ment we found that we had only a skunk and a
striped one at that, but we didn't lose heart at
that but kept right on, now and then changing
a trap or two.

At last one morning my partner said to me,
"I think I have found out what the trouble is
with our trapping." "That's good," I said, "tell
me about it." "Well," went on Dan, "you see
all the traps we've got set on that brook are
along the banks. Well now the stream is all
frozen over tight so that nothing can get into the
brook from the outside, so I don't see why a
mink coming up that brook under the ice — for
under the ice they must come or we would see

their tracks somewhere along the bank — can smell the bait on the outside, so what I think best is this: Take an axe and cut a long hole about 8 inches wide clear across the brook. Now get some sticks about 3 or 4 feet long, it all depends on the depth of the water, and drive them into the mud, beginning at one side of the brook. Now drive until you get to the middle of the brook, then do the same on the other side, leaving a place about the width of the trap in the middle. Care must be taken to get sticks near enough together so he can't get through only just at the middle. Now if the water is very deep so he can't get through only just at the middle, we can build up until about to the surface or say 4 inches from the surface. Now set your trap on the thing you have built up, and just between the posts, and I think you will have him."

This advice was acted upon at once and the next morning we had a fine mink measuring about 28 inches. The next morning we had another and in a few mornings another, and so on until we had caught just nine mink from that place.

Some trappers say it is hard to catch mink, others say that they are as easy to catch as muskrats. Now which is right? I believe here in Washington that where there are lots of quail, rabbits and other wild fowl that the mink is harder to catch with dead bait than he would be if game was more scarce. But that ought not to interfere with the mink being hard to catch. When he gets a warm meal he would be a fool to take cold and sometimes stale meat.

I will tell you the way I catch them when they refuse dead bait. First see that there are no broken links in your trap and that the jaws close together good, for many trappers never look to this and thereby lose a valuable pelt, and worst of all it teaches the mink to be more careful next time.

Now that you have your traps in order, go to some small stream where you see fresh mink tracks. Go up until you find there is a log across the creek, and nine times out of ten you will see where the mink go under the log, and now there is the place to nab him. First block up all space under the log so as to force the mink into the water, stones, stick or anything handy is good to stop their runway. Now set your trap in about two inches of water. If it is too deep shovel in some dirt and if too shallow dig a trench. Then fasten your chain to a sliding pole and your set is complete. Splash some water on the ground where you have stood and you have a good set that will catch mink.

Some say that mink are afraid of iron. Well

in some cases they are, but in others they are
not. For instance a mink goes out in search of
food and comes to a wire fence or a railroad
track. I do not think he will shy at that for he
is used to the smell of iron and rust at that
place. But jam an old rusty trap in his den and
not cover it or set a rusty trap under old rotten
bait. I don't think any mink will get caught
there. I catch as many mink with bait as without it, but when I bait I bait with strictly fresh
bait. Muskrat, quail, rabbits and fish are all
good baits. When I bait with muskrat I use the
glands for scent and fish oil when with fish. But
have the traps free from rust in all cases.

Go along a stream where the mink frequents
and look for holes in the bank, most of which are
made by the muskrat, and set the trap just on
the outside squarely in front of it, says an Iowa
trapper. Never set inside the hole. Now the
reason for this is that the mink will very often
just take a peep in and then go on, in which case
if the trap was set inside you would fail to get
him. When if it were on the outside you would
stand a chance. Then turn the spring to one
side and set the trap so the mink will step between the jaws and not over one, for in stepping
over them the jaw strikes the foot and throws it
upwards, catching by the end of the toe or fail-

ing to catch at all. Cover trap lightly and carefully, being careful not to get anything on the
jaws to hinder them from closing on the foot.

Another good set is at the root of a tree which
has a small hole in it. Set the trap the same as
at the hole in the bank. Still another is where
the muskrats got an opening through the ice or
frozen bank. Mr. Mink is always looking for
such places and is very easily caught at them. I
caught six mink in one week at a place of this
kind last winter, and would have caught still
more if the water hadn't spoiled the place. A
good way to kill a mink is to strike him on the
end of the nose and stove towards the eyes.
This will kill them quicker than pounding their
heads into a mush, and then the head is easily
skinned.

In regard to mink being afraid of human
scent, that is all nonsense, says a Maine trapper.
They are no more afraid of human scent than a
skunk, and every trapper knows that a skunk is
not. Now the way I catch mink mostly is in
ditches and springs and runs at the head of
marshes and around rivers and trout brooks.

Find a ditch and pick out a narrow place and
where the bank is quite steep on each side, so
that when a mink goes up and down he will have
to walk on the bottom of the ditch. Now get

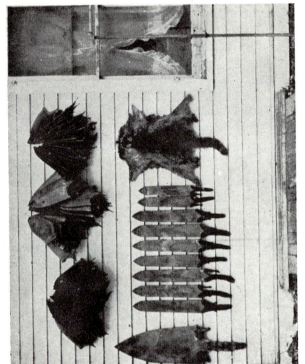

A FEW DAYS CATCH.

.ome dry sticks and begin on each side and stop up the ditch all but in the center, the bigness of a Blake & Lamb trap, have the sticks ten inches high and put them very close together, because a mink will go through a very small place.

Scoop out a hollow where the trap sets and be sure to set the trap with spring pointing straight up or down the ditch, because if it sets crossways and he steps on edge of pan, the jaw will knock the foot out of the trap. Now don't forget about setting the trap right and be sure to stop every little place so he will have to go over the trap. Do a good job and you are sure of your mink. You don't have to have any bait when you set this way.

Always keep your eyes open, look into every hole and ditch, and when you see mink tracks in a place that is the place to put your traps. I never fail to get them when I find signs of them. For the benefit of those who haven't a marsh or ditch this is another way that I use, and know it to be all right. Go along the brook and find the roots of an old tree in under the bank. Build a coop with sticks, bark or rocks, cover it over with stuff to make it tight. Make it eight inches long and wide enough so a trap will fill the entrance. Remember about the spring point- ing in or straight out. Hollow out a place for trap, and cover trap, chain and all, with fine dry grass leaves, and have the trap set level with the earth. Now for the bait, shoot a red squirrel and cut him open from one end to the other and hang him up in back end of coop, and you will get them if there are any around there.

I have used all kinds of bait including musk rats, fish, birds and chicken heads, but find squirrel to be the best. I have caught more mink with this bait than all the others put together. In setting traps for any animal be sure to set your trap as near as possible where they are in the habit of traveling. Some set down anywhere and think they ought to catch everything that comes along. You can read lots of ways of trapping but you can't learn it all. Experience and practice is what teaches any one to be a successful trapper, and when you learn anything yourself you know it to be a fact.

A mink, like a man, prefers dry footing when traveling up stream, says a Wisconsin trapper and will always run along on an old log if they can, in muddy places or across small bays along the bank of a stream. Find a place where a mink makes small detours around soft places and lay a chunk of log about 6 inches in diameter across the place. Put a trap on the end of it. Arrange it so he will have to make a long jump on the up stream end to reach hard footing. He will naturally put his foot as near to the end of the log as he can so as to make the jump, and you will have him. Use no bait or scent and leave no signs of your presence. Make the place look natural.

It was while running a line of traps up Deer Creek last November that mink got to disturbing my muskrat sets, says an Indiana trapper. Mr. Mink would wait until the muskrat drowned, then he would spoil the pelt. As usual, he got in his work rainy nights. One morning I found a rat pretty badly torn and I began scheming at once to catch the sly chap. I observed a shallow sand bar out in the middle of the creek, just in front of my set, so I laid my plans at once. I cut out a piece of sod one-half foot square, placed it on the sand bar; this made the water over the sod two inches deep. I now took the muskrat and placed him in the center of the piece of sod, putting his head under the water so he would not appear dangerous, as a mink is afraid of a large muskrat. I fixed him so that one half was under water and the other half above. I left the fur on, you understand, so as to make it appear more natural.

I now took four Newhouse No. 1 traps and placed one on each side of the rat, staked out in deep water, full length of chain, so anything caught in one trap would not disturb the others. I covered the traps well with water soaked leaves, the grass on the sod helping to cover traps some. You will observe that the traps are well concealed, being two inches under water. It is well to drive stakes out of sight under the water also. The next morning the set was not disturbed, but the following morning, it having rained some that night, I expected something was doing, and I was not disappointed, for on approaching the set I saw distinctly outlined beneath the water the dark forms of a mink and another muskrat, caught in two of the traps.

One mink I caught by placing an old rotten piece of wood on each side of a muskrat slide, close to the water. I then covered it over with the same material, leaving an opening at each end; then I placed a No. 1 Newhouse trap under the water at the mouth of the tunnel. Mr. Mink simply had to go through this runway, and of course was caught and drowned.

CHAPTER XV.

A good many trappers, both amateur and professional, speak of mink being hard to catch. I can't see it that way, says a Pennsylvania trapper. Really they are as easy as the water mole or skunk with me. I simply set all my traps bare, no covering whatever, you clog your trap when sprung. I lost a good many by so doing, so now I set bare at all times for both skunk and mink, and I get my share of them.

I use both bait and blind set; water set I think is the best, that is, in bitter cold weather when the ice is thick. My way of making, I call it the ice set, is to take a piece of oil cloth or an old buggy top cover will do, and put about five pounds of salt in same and sew up; have it about two inches thick. Don't make it too solid, leave it loose enough so you can work the most of the salt around the edges to bed trap in. Now puncture with needle to let fumes of salt through; cut a hole through the ice at the edge of the water, scrape out hole to bed salt in; but first put a stone in the hole, and bottom and side it up with stone to keep the mud from clogging the needle holes. Now you will wonder what the salt is for; simply to keep the ice from freezing the hole shut. I had nine of that kind of sets set last winter and trapped seven mink. The hole will never freeze shut. Always set trap under water.

Last winter I complained to my better half that I had better take my traps out of the run where I trap, as I couldn't make a water set because my traps froze over night. She said, why don't you put salt around your traps? That put me to thinking so I got an old piece of oil cloth and got her to make four for me on the sewing machine; I put a five pound sack of salt in each one.

The best place to set is on the inside of a curve. In slack water you will have to keep moving your set at the water rises and falls. Undoubtedly that is the best cold water set I have ever tried, and it has been a complete success with me.

I use the cubby set for mink. Before severe weather sets in I take two boards six or eight feet long, lean them against each other V shape, put water mole carcass (rabbit, chicken or fish is also good) in center and a trap at each end, about one foot from end. I also have the hollow log set. It is on the same principle as the cubby set. A cubby is easily built. You can make them out of stone if you can't get boards.

CHAPTER XVI.

LOG AND OTHER SETS.

My advice to all young trappers is, study the nature and habits of your game and you will be successful in taking all kinds of fur bearing animals. Here is one of my methods, writes a trapper, of taking mink around swamps and lakes where there are shallow springs that never freeze up.

The bait house: This should be built in about two inches of water, as follows: Get some sticks about one foot and a half long and drive one end in the mud in the shape of a horse shoe, with the tops leaned together and a door left in one side about three inches wide. The pen should be a foot wide. Now get some moss, grass or weeds (the moss from an old rat house is best) and cover over well. Lay a chip of chunk of wood back of the house and place a piece of fresh muskrat on it. Set the trap under water on the door with spring pointing to one side. If there is deep water near by the drowning wire is the best way to fasten traps, and if water is shallow fasten the trap to a long stone of about eight or ten pounds weight and place back as far as the chain will reach from the house.

There are certain springs around all lakes and swamps that a mink will visit every time that he comes that way, and if a house is made at these springs and kept baited every mink can be caught.

The bait hole: This is a good method to use along creeks and rivers before the water freezes over in the fall. Find a steep bank a foot or more high near the water and dig a hole back in a foot deep and about eight inches high and level with the water. Scoop the dirt out in front of the hole about two feet wide and two inches under the water; but don't get the hole so low as to let the water back in. Let the water come up to the mouth of the hole and set a No. 1 steel trap square in front of the entrance with the spring pointing away, and fasten so the mink will drown.

The log set: Find where an old log lies in the water, stick chunks of wood in under the log on the bank so the mink will have to pass around in the water under the log. Set trap, a No. 1, in an inch of water square under the log and stake out in deep water as far as possible. If a little bait is sprinkled on each side of the log it will hasten the capture of the mink.

The ditch set: Early in the season the mink

are great rovers and explore every ditch, hole or hollow log near the stream, and a trap set in the ditch in shallow water will often get one. If the ditch is too wide, drive a row of sticks across and leave an opening for the trap. Set the trap

THREE LOG SET.

in the opening and fasten it back as far as possible.

The dry log set: Mink have a habit of passing through every hollow log that lies near the stream and if one can be found like this it is a good place to catch them all winter. Put some bait back in the log and set your trap in the entrance. Cover the trap and chain with powdered rotten wood, sprinkle it all around near the trap, and fasten to a drag or small pole.

These five ways are the only methods I use. Sometimes I set a trap for a few nights where a mink travels around a small bog between the bog and the bank, and very often get one in these places.

In setting for mink on land I go about it in this way:

First, I prepare my traps by boiling in hemlock boughs. Before setting my trap I dig up the ground with a trap hook. Dig a place two feet across and set the trap in the middle and cover lightly with fine leaves, putting some under the trap to keep it from freezing to the ground.

Don't be afraid to dig up the ground thoroughly, as a mink will always stop and investigate such a place. Have your hook long enough so you will not have to walk on the new ground. Fasten your trap to a springy bush or brush-drag.

After the ground freezes you will have to shelter your traps. I have used the following ways with good success:

Take two good sized chunks of wood and lay them about six inches apart. Set a No. 1½ trap between them at each end, put your bait between the two traps and cover it with small brush and grass. If you can find an old hollow log it is a good place to set. These two sets you can use all winter.

Red squirrel, chicken, rabbit, partridge, muskrat or turtle are all good baits.

When you get a mink or rat alive let it bleed around your trap. It is also a good plan to hitch a string around your bait and drag it from one trap to another.

A man that follows the woods has some queer experiences, said a Pennsylvania trapper. Some eight or ten years ago I was hunting the Allegheny Mountains. It was in January and we were camped on the Elk River. There was a light snow on the ground. My trapping partner told me he would show me how to catch mink with the land set. Taking our traps we went down the river until we came to some logs that lay across a hollow. In some places the log was from three to four feet from the ground, and other places it was not over two feet. Sticks and limbs had lodged against the log, leaving small openings. In these open places we set our traps, covering them over with leaves. We caught several this way.

Now that will do in West Virginia, but in Pennsylvania in this part of the state it takes a water set or a deadfall to catch the mink. In the F-F-G I have seen a great many different opinions in regard to trapping mink, some claiming they have no trouble in catching mink, others cannot catch them only with the water set or deadfall.

Now my experience is that it depends upon where I am. In the sandhill region of Virginia I could catch mink only with the water set, while in the mountains they were very easily caught with the land set. Much depends on what kind of bait is used. I once had a line of eighteen traps baited with birds and chickens on the Nottoway River, and out of the eighteen traps, I baited one with the carcass of a muskrat. Well, I didn't catch any mink in the traps baited with chicken offal and birds but the trap baited with muskrat won.

CHAPTER XVII.

POINTS FOR THE YOUNG TRAPPER.

It is better for the novice to serve a few season's apprenticeship on the muskrat or skunk
before attempting the capture of the shrewder
fur bearing animals. Boys, if you live near a
trout brook, a creek, pond, bog or spring hole,
where there are fish, frogs or clams, you may be
sure that any such water is frequented, or at
least visited by mink, though your unpracticed
eyes may fail to detect signs of their presence;
and by procuring a few traps and setting them
according to some methods, you can realize a
good bit of pocket money every year, and at the
same time have more real pleasure than you get
from all other sports combined. Don't be discouraged if you catch nothing at first. Visit
your traps regularly, keep your eyes open and
your wits about you, be patient and persistent,
and success is bound to come in the end.

The young trapper's first essay for the mink
should be with some sort of water set—dry sets
requiring much greater skill and caution—and
of the many methods employed the following is
perhaps the most effective for one so simply con-

trived. Having chosen a suitable location for
your trap, preferably some good sized pool with
the water still and not too deep at the edge, and
the bank rising so abruptly that the set will not
easily be over-flowed; gather up a few dead
sticks 1½ inch thick and break into stakes about
15 inches long. Drive these firmly into the
ground to form a three-sided pen four inches
wide by eight inches long, the open side at the
water's edge.

Hollow out a little place for the trap and
place with the spring in line with the entrance,
as the animal's foot will then be less likely to be
thrown out by the jaws closing; press the chain
down into the mud out of sight; fix the ring pole,
running it well out into deep water; put the bait
(fish, bird or squirrel) in the pen, pinning securely with a dead stick, lay a few sticks over
top of pen, and cover trap carefully with rotten
leaves fished up from the bottom, dropping on a
few pinches of mud, and sticking a row of short
twigs on the outer side to keep them from
spreading or floating away. Then if the water
falls the trap will remain nicely covered.

You now have things pretty well in shape,
unless you apprehend trouble from trap thieves.
In such case you cannot conceal your set too
carefully, for a theft may not mean merely the
loss of a trap, but possibly a valuable pelt as

well. An excellent mode of concealment is to cut several fir, pine or hemlock shrubs and stick them up, as if growing about the pen, which is most likely to attract the eye. Also throw a scraggly top of some kind into the water over the ring-pole to hide the catch after drowning. Lastly, rearrange as naturally as possible the leaves and dead stuff disturbed in your work, see that nothing has fallen on the trap, spatter a little water about and your set is complete.

Another good way is to drop two traps side by side in shallow water, surround each by a little circle of rocks and hang the bait by a thread about 12 inches above them. In trying to reach the bait Mr. Mink runs a good chance of blundering into one of the traps.

Better yet, get a shallow box having a weather-worn appearance, bore half inch holes in the sides, and sink in the brook so that the water coming in through the holes will cover the bottom to a depth of three inches. Drape the sides with moss and weeds, put in some live trout and two or three traps along with them, and for those mink that are so particular as to want to take their food alive, you have a set that insures them a warm reception.

Yet another method is to find an over-hanging bank with a narrow strip of beach between it and the water. Beginning at the water, drive stakes at an acute angle out to the bank, both up and down the stream. At the apex of the V shaped fence thus formed place trap under water. No bait is needed.

I was speaking of water sets. One more and I will pass on to the land set, for though an almost endless variety of the former could be given those presented, with such modifications as will suggest themselves under varying conditions, will serve as a very good elementary education for the young trapper. The following was given me by an old trapper: We were riding together near a brook when he said, "I set a trap here three years ago, which I have never had an opportunity to visit, but I will wager you there is a mink in it if it is to be found." Whereupon he left me for a few minutes, returning triumphantly with the trap and the skeleton of a mink's foot in the jaws.

His way was to go along to shallow riffles, pin a piece of meat to the bottom, place the trap a few inches below it, and a little above drive a short line of stakes at right angles to the current to keep off drift. High water or low, cold weather or warm, you were sure, he asserted, of every mink that came up or down the stream. And my own experience has gone very far towards making this claim good.

Now, all of the foregoing sets are easily

made, and may be used by the novice, after a little practice, with every probability of fair success, but when we leave the water for dry land
greater difficulties will be encountered. There
is a smell about iron which wild animals are
quick to detect and recognize as an indication of
danger. Water destroys this scent, but of
course in the land set this advantage is lost.

Various directions were given for killing it
by smoking or steeping, but I have found that if
the trap be properly covered there is small need
of spending time in this way. And right here let
me say that in dry sets success hinges largely on
the skill with which you cover your trap, especially if bait be used, and it is best to use bait
until one has gained a pretty good idea of the
habits of his game. The bait may be protected
by a pen of stakes such as is described in my
first water set, but placed a little back from the
water in as dry a place as possible.

At the entrance dig a cavity somewhat
larger than a trap, with a shallow trench leading around to one side for chain. Line with fine
sprigs of hemlock, and set trap evenly and
firmly. The hemlock will not only keep trap
and chain from freezing down (a thing to be
carefully avoided) but also help to neutralize
that tell-tale smell of metal. Get some moss of
a dry fibrous nature and containing no earthly

matter to freeze. That found on rocks is generally the best. Tear out a crescent-shaped piece
of a size to half fill trap, and fitting snugly between pan and jaw and two small pieces to fill
in on back or trigger side of pan — or only one
piece, like the first, if using a trap with spring
on the outside.

If you have done your work properly, the inside of the trap is completely filled, from jaws
to pan, with no chance for anything to get under
the pan, and no wad of batting beneath it (as is
used by some) to become swollen with moisture
and prevent its free working. Now go around
trap on the outside with moss, pressing it in so
as nearly to cover jaws, lay a thin leaf over pan,
and cover with well pulverized rotten wood,
which may be found in any old stump.

Lastly, throw on bits of leaf and pinches of
dirt until it resembles as nearly as possible the
surrounding ground. Don't be afraid of covering too heavily, so long as you don't put too
much over hinges or jaws. You want it so that
the iron will not be washed bare with the first
rain. But avoid any appearance of a mound, as
nothing arouses an animal's suspicions quicker
than this. The chain may be covered with loose
earth and stump dust. Some advise hitching to
a clog, but I generally use a stake, and seldom
ever lose a mink by footing. But if a green stake

is used be careful to smear the exposed end with mud to remove its fresh appearance, and to secure the bait use a dead stick invariably.

Many guide books speak of leaves as a covering for the trap, but the fact is that dry leaves are something that the mink habitually avoids, doubtless not liking the rustling sound given out in traveling over them; hence it is best to use them in land sets sparingly, and to locate your trap so that the shy fellow will not have to wallow through a carpeting of them to reach it

I have had excellent luck by placing trap at the edge of a bank a foot or so high, with a good runway underneath. The mink smells the bait from below and springing up to investigate often lands plump in the trap, when if he had been afforded the chance for a closer inspection he might have gone on without troubling it. You may think this a small thing, but it is just such trifles that circumvent the shy fellows.

In making your set do all the work from the back side; also approach on the same side when visiting. Go no nearer than necessary to see that everything is all right, and make your stay in the vicinity as short as possible. If any part of the trap has become exposed cover with stump dust. A small fir stuck down by the trap with branches projecting over it will serve as a

protection from rain and snow, but is seldom
needed when trap is covered as above described.

Always be on the lookout for places to set
when hunting or fishing. Let your eyes run
along the strips of beach and boggy, peer under
overhanging banks and among piles of drift, and
scrutinize closely every log spanning streams.
You will be surprised to find how often you will
hit upon footprints, droppings, holes and runways, the knowledge of which will be of the ut-
most value to you when the trapping season ar-
rives.

If you trap the same section year after year
you will get to know the favorable points at the
beginning, and get much better results at that;
for one trap in the right place is worth a dozen
clapped down haphazzard. Some places are
good for one or more mink every year; an old
hollow log near the water, a passageway among
roots or under a fallen tree trunk, a narrow
shelf along the face of the bluff, a particular
hole or den — any of these, if kept guarded by
a well set trap, may prove a little bonanza for
you every season. In such places it is better to
use no bait, a little fish oil perhaps excepted, as
you will then take unawares many a sly old fellow to whom a morsel of meat, no matter how
cunningly arranged, would be simply a sign-
board of danger.

SOME NEW YORK STATE SKINS.

I remember well my first experience at this style of trapping mink. I noticed what looked to be a well worn little path on the bank of a stream leading down under a big pile of drift. As an experiment I placed a trap in this path, and to my delight found a fine mink waiting for me at my next visit. Two more mink followed within a week in the same place, while a trap nearby carefully set and baited was not molested.

I had supposed I knew about all there was to trapping, but this opened my eyes a bit. I began searching out and setting in similar places, with the result that my usual catch was doubled that season. One day on looking into a hole which had rotted into the foot of a big ash standing on the bank of a stream I saw a small dead fish lying among the roots as if it had been left there by some creature that had taken itself off at my approach. I promptly clapped two traps into the cavity, taking care not to disturb the fish, and soon after had a mink as a reward for my trouble.

But the best natural situation I ever discovered was under a high, overhanging bank — just the sort of roadway every mink coming along that side of the stream would be sure to choose — at a point where a willow tree completely blocked the way, except for a narrow passage perforating its tangled roots.   One trap could guard this effectually, and, as in the trunk of the old ash, it was entirely protected from snow or rain.   Of course a mink could get around the trunk by taking to the water, but so far as I could judge they seldom did so, and each year as long as there were any mink in the vicinity I was sure of several here.

Mink in fact prefer traveling by land as a rule.   For this reason a trap placed at either end of a log spanning a stream that is too wide for them to jump forms a most killing set.   Drive a few stakes on each side of a log at the ends to prevent the animal from jumping shore to one side of trap, and use extra strong traps, as you are likely to drop on a fox or coon with this set. No bait is needed.   In winter any spring hole, even if near human habitations, offers good possibilities.   Mink visit them to burrow for frogs, and one or two traps sunk in the mud and shallow water are pretty sure of an occasional catch. And they are but little trouble to tend as the warm spring water prevents freezing.

Now a word about bait.   In my opinion the very best bait is fish; trout, pickerel, shiner or any other fresh fish, being all about equally good.   But salt fish should never be used for mink, though after being smoked it makes a taking bait for coon.   Red squirrel I consider next

to fish. They are plentiful everywhere, and the
mink makes many a meal off of them in the absence of his favorite food. The oft-quoted chick-
en's head has invariably failed for me, nor have
I found the flesh of the muskrat such a killer as
is claimed by some. Partridge heads, wood mice
and frogs are all good. In the absence of anything else I have sometimes used English spar-
rows with fair results.

Don't be too generous with your baits. A
section of small fish an inch long is sufficient
and much less likely to arouse suspicions than a
larger piece. In carrying bait in your bag, wrap
in an old rag so it will not come in contact with
the metal of hatchet or traps, and wash clean
before using. Locate your traps on long, com-
paratively straight reaches of the stream, as
mink often make short cuts when traveling and
might miss your set entirely if placed on a bend.
Above all, study your game and don't get too
knowing to take a pointer.

CHAPTER XVIII.

PROPER SIZE TRAPS.

For mink I have found a No. 0 trap, if carefully set with proper precaution, is as good and lucky as a No. 1 or 1½ trap as some trappers advocate, writes a Canadian trapper. I used a bunch on a considerable sized lake one fall. The lake had numerous small creeks and rivers falling into it. At the junction of these with the lake I set my traps. They were all No. 0, selected on account of their lightness, as there was a long carry to get to the lake from a traveled route and added to the canoe, my gun, blanket and provisions, the traps were somewhat of a consideration, and I therefore took the ones of less weight.

I made two visits to the lake before it froze and got 20 mink, 1 marten and a female fisher.

Where I made a water set I saw that the water outside went down pretty bold, and I always tied a stone to the trap and thus insured the animal drowning.

Where I set on land I without fail attached the chain to a tossing pole, thereby preventing the fur being damaged by mice or the animal being eaten by some other.

Some may question the possibility of such small traps being for any length of time in order as a water set, but I must explain. The lake was of considerable size and the season the latter part of October. Such a lake at that season of the year is not subject to any great fluctuations in the height of the water.

I may say in conclusion about this particular sized trap, that on that trapping tour I only lost one mink. I found the trap sprung with a single toe in the jaws.

The trap had been a dry set one, and by reading the signs I found some snow had melted and dripped from an over-hanging branch on to the junction of the jaws. This had frozen (the trap being in the shade) and prevented its usual activity. As a consequence it only caught on as the mink was in the act of lifting his foot, so I was satisfied it was circumstance and not the fault of the trap that caused the missing of this mink.

The No. 1 Blake & Lamb and the Oneida Jump are the ideal mink traps for me, says an Ohio trapper. When it comes to the snow set the old Blake & Lamb is second to none. The only fault I find with this trap is that the chain is not long enough, and this is the fault with other makes of traps as well.

When I trap mink I use muskrat carcass for

water sets. The favorite food of the mink is crawfish, frogs and fish. Of course this kind of bait can't well be found in the trapping season. When I find a sly old mink I leave off both scent and bait, conceal my traps well under the bank or places where it likely travels, and just leave the trap there. If I don't catch it in a week I only go close enough to see whether there is anything in the trap or not.

About mink, I think they are queer little animals. Sometimes they are wise and sometimes they are not. I think the reason some of them are wise is because they get educated on trap lore by getting their toes pinched in some poor trap or trap that is carelessly set. I use No. 1 Newhouse for mink and lost only one mink out of my traps last season, and I got one of his toes. I cover my traps so there isn't a bit of chain or trap in sight, and use clean traps free from rust. I use muskrat musk and mink musk with a good success, but common sense is the best.

I trapped over the same ground all winter and caught four mink in one place and three in another. I see that some trappers think that the scent of the mink will scare them away, but that is the best scent I could find when trapping mink on rat houses. A large rat will make a hard fight for a small mink if he has a fair show, and when a mink gets into a fight he will throw out scent like a skunk. For that reason I think scent is all right to attract mink to traps.

Now if you set a trap and use this scent with a little muskrat musk, when a mink comes along he smells the musk of both mink and rat, and begins to look around or rather smell around for the remains of the rat to make a meal on. If you have the trap and scent in the right place you will have another mink on your list.

Of course there are a few old fellows that are educated that are pretty shy of anything that isn't natural to them. These fellows you can catch in blind sets somewhere along your line. About the best place I can find to catch mink is where they drill into a rat house to catch rats. They smell around till they find a soft place on the south side of the house and dig a hole just large enough to crawl through, right into the rat's nest.

CHAPTER XIX.

DEADFALLS.

First a little pen about a foot square is built of stones and chunks or by driving stakes close together, leaving one side open. The pen should be built smaller and tighter than shown in illustration, so that a small mink or weasel cannot get in from the back or sides. The pen in illustration is purposely large so that triggers and bait can be seen, giving the inexperienced deadfall trapper a better idea of how to set.

The stakes should be cut about thirty inches long and driven into the ground some sixteen inches, leaving fourteen, or thereabout above the ground. Of course if the earth is very solid stakes need not be so long, but should be so driven that only about fourteen inches remains above ground. A sapling say four inches in diameter and four feet long is laid across the end that is open. A sapling that is four or five inches in diameter and about twelve feet long is now cut for the "fall."

Stakes are set so that this pole or fall will play over the short pole on the ground. These stakes should be driven in pairs; two about

eighteen inches from the end; two about fourteen further back. (See illustration). The
small end of the pole should be split and a stake
driven firmly through it so there will be no danger of the pole turning and "going off" of its
own accord.

The trap is set by placing the prop (which is
only seven inches in length and half an inch
through) between the top log and the short one
on the ground, to which is attached the long
trigger, which is only a stick about the size of
the prop, but about twice as long, the baited end
of which extends back into the little pen. The
figure 4 triggers can be used if preferred, but
the two piece is as good if not better. The bait
may consist of a piece of fish, chicken, rabbit or
any tough bit of meat so long as it is fresh, and
the bloodier the better.

An animal on scenting the bait will reach
into the trap — the top of the pen having been
carefully covered over — between the logs.
When the animal seizes the bait the long trigger is pulled off of the upright prop and down
comes the fall, killing the animal by its weight.
Skunk, coon, opossum, mink, and in fact nearly
all kinds of animals are easily caught in this
trap. The fox is an exception, as it is rather
hard to catch them in deadfalls.

The more care you take to build the pen tight

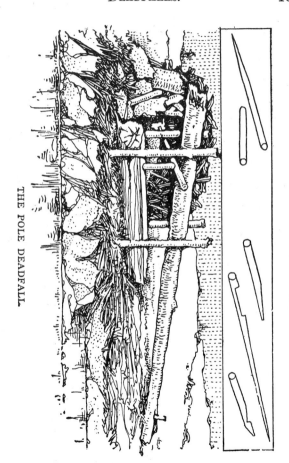

THE POLE DEADFALL.

and strong the less liable is some animal to tear it down and get the bait from the outside; also if you will cover the pen with leaves, grass, sticks, etc., animals will not be so shy of the trap. The triggers are very simple, the long one being placed on top of the upright, or short one. The long trigger should have a short prong left or a nail driven in it to prevent the game from getting the bait off to easy. If you find it hard to get saplings the right size for a fall, and are too light, they can be weighted with a pole laid on the "fall."

The most successful trapper uses some deadfalls as well as steel traps, especially if trapping for a season at one place. If trapping season after season in the same locality deadfalls are a great help for mink that are apparently hard to catch in steel traps readily take bait from deadfalls and get caught. On the other hand, mink that refuse to take bait from deadfalls are often caught in blind steel trap sets.

The experienced trapper knows that mink travel along creeks, rivers, swamps, ponds and lakes. Care should be taken in selecting places to build deadfalls. If there are dens this is a good place to construct them. If there are many dens so much the better, but one is all that is required, for a mink is apt to investigate all and will scent bait. If you are acquainted with the territory you must know some places where mink frequent. It seems that the nature and habits of mink are such that although a mink had never traveled that territory before it would follow about the same course as others, as tracks in the mud and snow showed.

To prove this I will mention that some years ago in one deadfall I caught eight mink in five winters and one in a steel trap, making nine caught in the five years. This deadfall was built on the bank of a small stream some 20 feet from the water and near a large sycamore, under which there was a den, although the trap was some feet from the entrance to the den.

The first winter one mink was taken; the second two; the third three; the fourth two; the fifth one.

The fourth winter a few weeks after catching one in the deadfall the trap was down and the bait gone. The trap was rebaited, but for several trips I found the trap down and bait eaten. I felt sure that it was a mink, and although I set the triggers easy—I was using the two piece trigger and upright spindle—the animal continued to get the bait.

After a few more visits and the trap down, bait invariably eaten, I made the pen smaller. The next round I brought a No. 1 Newhouse

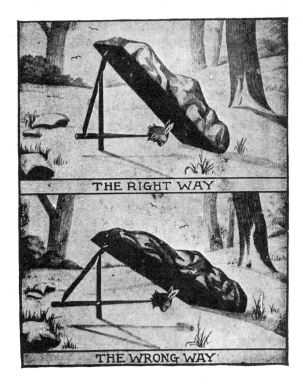

STONE DEADFALLS.

steel trap intending to set it if the deadfall was down without making a catch. Sure enough it was.

For some trips I had been suspecting that the "bait getter" was a small mink. I baited and reset the deadfall as usual. Next a small place was excavated inside the pen and near the bait, on the deadfall spindle, the trap placed and carefully covered.

The next morning I found everything as I had left it the day before, but the second round I saw that the "fall" was down before I got near and on closer approach saw a mink, a very small one, in the steel trap.

The mink was small and went inside the pen for the bait. In constructing deadfalls for mink care must be taken to have the pen built tight but not too large.

It is best to build deadfalls in advance of the active trapping season so that the animals may become accustomed to them, and the trap weather beaten. Chopping and pounding might tend to drive animals away. In August, September and October is a good time to build, for if in new territory signs, if any, should be readily seen.

While it is best to construct deadfalls in advance of trapping season, yet the writer has built deadfalls late in November, set and baited and found mink in them the next morning. If rightly built ten or a dozen is all a man can make in a day, and like setting steel traps, a dozen carefully set for mink are worth a hundred set at haphazzard.

Mink are great travelers, so that it is needless to set deadfalls close together. One about every mile is enough unless there should be many dens and rocky bluffs along the streams, then they could to advantage be built closer, for other game is liable to be caught. In this case they should be made a little heavier, as you may catch opossum, skunk and coon.

Where one stream empties into another is often a good place to construct a deadfall. If before selecting your places to build a few trips are taken along the stream it will be a great help. Where small streams empty into ponds or lakes or the outlets will be found ideal places for mink.

When the deadfalls are built before the trapping season it is well to set them, having the top of the pen covered, just as though the trap was baited and ready for business.

Another thing that should be carefully looked after is triggers. Many cut triggers from green bushes. If this is done, hard wood such as oak, hickory, dogwood, sugar, beech, etc., is best. The upright trigger, which is only a straight piece of

wood about a half inch thick, should be slightly
rounded so that the spindle will slip off easier
when the animal is at bait.

It is a good idea to prepare a lot of triggers
in advance. For stone deadfalls the figure 4
must be used as the two piece will not work—
going off entirely too hard.

Of course we all admit the steel trap is more
convenient and up-to-date, says a New Hampshire trapper. You can make your sets faster
and can change the steel trap from place to
place. Of course the deadfall you cannot. But
all this does not signify the deadfall is no good;
they are good, and when mink trapping is con-
sumed the deadfall is the trap you want. To
the trapper who traps in the same locality every
year, when his deadfalls are once built it is only
a few minutes work to put them in shape, then
he has got a trap for the season.

I give a diagram of a deadfall (called here
Log Trap) which, when properly made and
baited, there is no such a mink catcher in the
trap line that has yet been devised. This trap
requires about twenty minutes time to make,
and for tools a camp hatchet and a good, strong
jack-knife, also a piece of strong string, which
all trappers carry. This trap should be about
fifteen inches wide with a pen built with sticks
or pieces of boards driven in the ground. (See

diagram.)   The jaws of this trap consist of two
pieces of board three inches wide and about
three and a half feet long, resting edgeways one
on the other, held firmly by four posts driven in
the ground.   The top board or drop should move

BOARD OR LOG TRAP.

easily up and down before weights are put on.
The treadle should be set three inches inside,
level with the top of bottom board.   This is a
round stick about three-fourths inch through
resting against two pegs driven in the ground.
(See diagram.)   The lever should be the same

size. Now put your stout string around top board, then set, pass lever through the string over the cross piece and latch it in front of the treadle, then put on weights and adjust to spring, heavy or light as desired. This trap should be set around old dams or log jams by the brook, baited with fish, muskrat, rabbit or chicken.

Home Tanning and Leather Making Guide

A Book of Information for Those Who Wish to Tan and Make Leather from Cattle, Horse, Calf, Sheep, Goat, Deer and Other Hides and Skins; Also Explains how to Skin, Handle, Classify and Market

THE author, Mr. Albert B. Farnham, is a Tanner and Taxidermist of more than 25 years' experience and who says: "Nothing in this book but what has been tested" — tried out by tanning one or two hides at a time, as well as several, therefore all methods given are practical.

Farmers, Ranchers, Butchers, Dairymen and others wanting to tan one or more hides, whether cattle, horse, calf, sheep, goat, deer, dog, woodchuck, squirrel, alligator, etc., for their own use or sale, can do so by following instructions as plainly given in this book. Why sell hides cheap and pay dear for leather or to have tanning done. MAKE MORE MONEY TANNING FOR OWN USE OR SALE.

This practical guide book, about 200 pages, 40 illustrations, 20 chapters, explains fully Alum, Chrome, Acid, Bark and Indian tanning methods. If Indians were able to tan buffalo, deer and other kinds into serviceable leather with next to no tools, surely with those you have and instructions as given in this book, should produce a good article — like the old time country tanner turned out.

Read the chapter headings which will show you how complete the book is:

This book is not only a GUIDE to tanning and leather making but also explains (with numerous illustrations) how to skin and handle to get highest prices for either hides or leather when sold.

Price, postpaid, paper bound, $3.00

A. R. Harding Pub. Co.   2878 E. Main St.—Columbus, Ohio 43209

Ginseng and Other Medicinal Plants

**A Valuable Book for Growers and Collectors of Wild Medicinal Plants
—Tells How to Grow, Medicinal Uses, Etc.**

THIS book, Revised Edition, contains 367 pages and about 100 illustrations, 40 being Ginseng, showing this plant in various stages of development, both cultivated and wild; also roots of different sizes and quality with explanation of value, etc. Also 20 illustrations of Golden Seal, showing plants and roots at different stages of growth. About 160 pages are devoted to Ginseng and more than 50 to Golden Seal—all of interest to growers, diggers and sellers. Some 40 other roots, plants and herbs having medicinal value are shown and briefly described. The raising of not only GINSENG and GOLDEN SEAL (the wild supply of which is nearly gone) but others as well are proving profitable.

This book contains Thirty-five chapters as follows:

Among the Plants described in Chapters XXVII to XXXV and which furnish Root Drugs are: Male Fern; Wild Turnip; Skunk Cabbage; Sweet Flag; Helonias; American Hellebore; Aletris; Bethroot; Wild Yam; Serpentaria (Southern Snakeroot); Yellow Dock; Soapwort; Goldthread; Oregon Grape; Twinleaf; Canada Moonseed; Bloodroot; Hydrangea; Indian Physic; Wild Indigo; Crane's Bill; Stillinga; Wild Sarsaparilla; Water Eryngo; American Angelica; Yellow Jasmine; Pinkroot; American Colombo; Black Indian Hemp; Pleurisy Root; Comfrey; Stoneroot; Culver's Root; Dandelion; Queen-of-the-Meadow; Elecampane; Echinacea; Burdock. *A good photograph of each is shown with the description.* Considerable money can be made collecting and preparing for the market. This book explains.

Price, postpaid, paper bound, $4.00

A. R. Harding Pub. Co.   2878 E. Main St.—Columbus, Ohio 43209